PHAETHON

PHAETHON

A STORY FOR

OUR MYTHIC MOMENT

F. Gard Jameson, PhD

Edited and Designed by

Dana C. White, PhD

COPPER CAULDRON PUBLISHING

Phaethon: A Story For Our Mythic Moment

First published 2009

ISBN: 978-0-615-28961-8 7

COPPER CAULDRON PUBLISHING

Typeset in the following fonts: Adobe Bembo Std, Cronos Pro, Herculaneum, Monotype Corsiva, and Papyrus.

Printed and bound by Toppan Printing Company (Shenzhen)

Text paper: 157 gsm Gold East gloss coated

Endsheets: 140 gsm Royal Elephant Woodfree

Case: Exceline

ISBN 978-0-615-28961-8

9 780615 289618

The Ride of Phaethon Begins
Ceiling Fresco
Galleria Uffizi – Florence, Italy

TABLE OF CONTENTS

The Chariot of Apollo, c.1905-14
Odilon Redon (1840-1916)
Musee d'Orsay - Paris, France

Introduction

Dennis Patrick Slattery, PhD

Myth is both ubiquitous and slippery—two major imperatives for its study. Myths insist on multiple levels of reading simultaneously even as they seek to be relevant over time, circumstance and historical differences. Such is their power and persistent energy.

For many years I considered myths to be stories: narratives of a particular people living in a particular time. But I no longer believe that is sufficient. Rather, mythologics plumb deeper waters of the psyche to reveal perennial patterns of energy, modalities of energy fields, sluices of consciousness in energic folds that uncover something more primal than story, before story, antedating narratives yet giving them their inner consistency. As such, the patterns of consciousness itself are given form when the energy folds of myth find their narrative similitude. Then the story becomes the vehicle for the myth that itself lies deep underground in the aquifer of consciousness, seeking release when the history of a period calls it forward, up and out. Myth, then, is intimately related to history, has a historical bouquet whenever it surfaces.

Richard Heinberg, influenced by the work of the seminal mythologist of our era, Joseph Campbell, follows the contours of the latter's thought in asserting that myths are "allegories for inner processes of spiritual transformation—that is as stories that are symbolically but never factually 'true.'"(14) True enough; and yet Campbell's works consistently reveal a strong historical or "euhemerist current" that demonstrates the factual or historical relevance of mythic stories, and that real events in real time often precipitated or coaxed such a narrative out of the reservoir of primal energy to express in imaginal form that actual event.

I like Heinberg's conclusion on this ostensible duality between myth and history: "When we examine myth and history closely the dividing line between the two becomes ever more faint and ambiguous." (16) He goes on to affirm that "Historiography originated in myth" (16) by revealing how Herodotus, the first modern historian, wrote factual narratives of the Persian wars, but did not stop with the actual battles; he pushed back further to reveal the origins of the conflict that began with the divinities and Titans of Olympus (16).

Because myths are at once historical and timeless, they can bleed from one cultural historical period to another when their analogical force seems most apparent. Such a move is what the mythologist F. Gard Jameson has done. He has discovered a confluence of myth and history in our own time by turning to this powerful story from Ovid's *Metamorphoses* as a way to see deeply into our modern crises. Moreover, he successfully balances in his study the matter of the myth and the metaphors that grow directly from it by tapping it on four levels, as he relates in the *Prologue*: "the literal, the thoughtful, the heartfelt, and the spiritual, which appeal to and evoke response from the body, the mind, the heart and the soul," (22) which remembers and extends an ancient form of reading, *Lectio Divina*. This setting the table to feast on such a myth is crucial, for this form of reading is not concerned with mastery and analysis as much as it is with contemplation and meditation, with imagining the myth into a new context that, paradoxically, is already inchoate in the original story.

The myth of *Phaethon*, like all myths, when contemplated rather than assessed, experienced deeply rather than explained, affords an opening into a higher and deeper level of consciousness, to reveal impulses in history that are mythic and to grasp the mythological energy moiling in the contemporary collective psyche, energies that can propel attitudes of excess, consumption, lack of expertise or training, absence of moderation, loss of a centered respect for the natural order and its limits, a certain recklessness that harbors hubris with ignorance and, finally, the living reality of the power inherent in the human species to exhaust or burn up the planet as our collective habitation.

Underneath the skin of the book, moreover, is another tale wanting to be told. Jameson's text prompts this reflection in me, the reader: What is it to see or understand mythically? What are its benefits? What is deepened and broadened by my exposure to myth? And finally, what kind of knowledge issues from seeing by means of a mythic story?

I would say, in venturing an answer to all of these queries, that the author sees through the myth to culture, sees by means of myth to history, and sees into the invisible workings of the heart by means of the narrative that opens an aperture into our cultural landscape. As readers, we are allowed to see by means of the myth, see by its style and manner of presentation, see by means of its imagery in a way that transcends logos or logical analysis. The myth moves us instead to a sublime understanding of what motivates and feeds the impulse of recklessness in the soul. Hubris, *Phaethon* reveals in successive iterations, is the soul's primal habitus.

Before I go on, I want to pause at this juncture to remark on the superb and attractive photos, prints, drawings, and paintings that appear on almost every page of Jameson's study. As I grow a bit riper, I so appreciate pictures in books, illustrations, even diagrams that can add to the intellect's understanding through words. The paintings of William Blake, sketches by Michelangelo, photos of the Buddha, Einstein, whorled seashells, photos of reliefs from Greek and Roman statuary, paintings through the centuries of Phaethon's violent end, photos of the planet—all of these and more provide a rich platter from which to feast. Often such delicacies are mentioned at the end of an introduction or a review; I want to include it here, for its aesthetic power cannot be overestimated. More images in books, please!

Now back to the language of this original study: without literalizing the mythology of *Phaethon*, Jameson skillfully reveals modern versions and visions of the young man's impulsive desire to drive the chariot of fire across the morning sky into evening, a task he is neither prepared for nor suited to accomplish with the skills and the maturity necessary for such a feat. But the author does relate Phaethon's recklessness to his uncertain and unstable relation with his father, Apollo. He reveals similarities in father-son relationships with various physicists and specifically with those who helped to create the atomic and hydrogen bombs.

What I enjoyed about Jameson's approach is his ability to discern the myth in the matter, to distill some essential and important truths from a close and sensitive reading of the original narrative, and to apply these truths to the moment at hand. What begins with a relationship between father and son is the genesis for a holocaust that can disintegrate the planet. That the earth is feminine thickens this intricate family plot that all myths, sooner or later, pull into their orbit.

The chariot of fire of nuclear power, its reins in the wrong hands, has the capacity to end life as we know it now, around the globe. Jameson writes: "...our western cultural value systems and mythologies are carrying us into a story that reads like the script of *Phaethon*." (79) Coupling Phaethon with Narcissus, the mythic figure who worships his own reflected self-image, the author sees in them both, victims as it were of the cult of the individual, the inherent danger "against excessive self-reference." Within such a landscape of narrow vision, the individual has the capacity and the propensity to turn the self into a deity, to canonize behavior that, when envisioned in a larger context, would be foolishness, but understood from the self-referential geography, seems both harmless and exciting. Such an attitude, Jameson suggests, can – and has today – become a world view shared by entire cultures and civilizations.

One antibody to such a diseased imagination, Jameson suggests, is to revisit the story of our cultural and historical time and to ask about its own limitations. If too narrow, then to work as a communal psyche "to see ourselves within the context of a much larger story, the story of the universe itself." (88) Broadening the plot line might indeed aid us in holding the line on species extinction, resource exhaustion, financial bankruptcy and global entropy. If myths in general, and the myth of *Phaethon* in particular, are entered into with the imagination that the author promotes, we can easily see Phaethon's appearance every day in our news media. Phaethon is unleashed into the contemporary series of crises in which individual greed and covetousness has promoted the loss of the chariot's reins. Every day the plunge is causing loss of home, job and savings and a carefully blueprinted future. I do not believe Jameson could have chosen a more relevant and prescient myth to explore in our current blights and plights that seem to be spreading globally.

Another quality that I admire about this meditation is the wide ranging disciplines that Jameson has a fine knowledge of, for example: theology, poetry, physics, science, biology, world mythology, cultural criticisms, depth and archetypal psychologies. Just scan the footnotes to see the footprints of such a wide path. Now this is an important observation, for it reveals and canonizes the study of mythology as a way into all other disciplines, so universal, to my mind, is the mythic imagination. It is not that the myth contains them all as much as the mythic narrative provokes them all through the fundamental power of analogy.

I want to italicize this idea: myths offer us ways to increase our powers of analogy, of seeing the figural in the literal, the metaphor imbedded in the matter; it is in short to develop a mytho-poetic sensitivity and openness to the narrative before us, within us and surrounding us. Such, for me, is the deeper value of such a study as Jameson's. My sense is that his deepening and wide-ranging inquiry could be done with any of the myths offered to us from the deep past. It shatters the notion or the silly question: "of what use is it to study literature, mythology, poetry? It can't get you a good-paying job!" Such is the anemic response to the study of mythology, one which Jameson's book smashes like an atom and releases the energy for all of us to see more, by means of myth.

I bring this Introduction to a close by reiterating a quote from Albert Einstein that Jameson cites beyond the midpoint of his study: "Imagination is more important than knowledge. For knowledge is limited, whereas imagination embraces the entire world, stimulating progress, giving birth to evolution." (159) From my reading, I believe that Einstein's quote serves as a bedrock for this study; something therapeutic is engaged in imagining in the way Einstein suggests. In the embrace is the epic impulse to inclusivity, to birthing the new within the decay of what has gone before; fertility is through the past, not through the arrogance of the narrow present. What we are learning from our own recent elections is that the world hungers not for another Phaethon but for a wider vision--epic, inclusive, moderate and sustaining. It is a new set of archetypes to replace and readjust the hungry desire of self-satisfaction. In such a transformation idols yield to icons.

Jameson ends his study by outlining what he terms the "three ages of cosmic time," influenced in part by the thought of spiritual ecologist Thomas Berry and astrophysicist Brian Swimme: the Age of Biological Evolution, the Age of Individuality and now, the Ecozoic Age. Only by seeing our dilemma within such vast categories can we perhaps grasp the more universal boundaries of our current plight as well as the opportunities imbedded in it. If we can adapt our desires and appetites to the third age, the Ecozoic, wherein we accept that "we are under the control of a super-ordinate Self, the divine nature of the cosmos," (212) then we can shift the paradigm away from the individual to a more communal world of largesse. The vision is not utopian or sentimental, New Age or quirky. In fact, it is the most realistic appraisal of hope one can imagine. All of this, out from under the flaming wheels of a chariot that toppled to earth so we can imagine it anew.

Dennis Patrick Slattery, Ph.D.

New Braunfels, Texas
November 12, 2008

Sources:
Heinberg, Richard. *Memories and Visions of Paradise: Exploring the Universal Myth of a Lost Golden Age.* Wheaton, Ill.: Quest Books, 1995.

Jameson, F. Gard. *Phaethon: A Story for Our Mythic Moment.*

I dedicate this book

to

my wife and muse, Florence,

and

my beloved children, Michael and Julia.

The Fall of Phaethon
Sebastiano Ricci (1659-1734)
Museo Civico - Belluno, Italy

PROLOGUE

P haethon - son of Apollo, the Sun God - convinced his father to let him drive the Chariot of Fire. But, inexperienced, unprepared, and filled with reckless bravado, Phaethon cannot control the horses. He crashes and burns. He lost control of the chariot, destroying the Earth and himself.

What can this ancient myth tell us about our world today? Like so many myths, the ancient story of *Phaethon* uses fiction to illuminate truth. It speaks to our divine heritage: the awesome gift of freedom, the temptations that come with our privilege, and our unwise use of that gift. Our failure to appreciate this heritage exacts a toll — costing us our humility and our wisdom, steering the short and turbulent human story into chapter after chapter of suffering. Some may say life is tragic, a farce without meaning. Epic literature affirms the tragic dimension of suffering in existence, but it also suggests hope, meaning, and numerous paths of illumination. Even in the darkest hours of a Nazi concentration camp, psychologist Victor Frankl could proclaim the meaningful depths of existence and the critical importance of an authentic search for that depth.

In the story of *Phaethon*, the "hero" gains control over the power of the Sun prematurely. He loses control, destroying himself and devastating the world in the process - graphically illustrating how it is that pride goes before the fall. Our relatively recent technological understanding and apparent control of the powers of the universe have positioned us on the brink of ecological devastation and further human grief. Can we step back from that brink? Are we able to learn the art of self-mastery? Is it even in our nature? At this moment in time, these questions arguably represent humankind's most pressing issues. The answers do not lie in the realm of political, economic or scientific solutions, but in reclaiming the enchantment of existence, a recovery of our intimate connection to our divine heritage.

A multitude of mythic images of that divine heritage have been cast by the prophets of old, both East and West, whether it be Apollo – the Sun God, the biblical Creator God, or Vishnu – the God of Incarnation. David Miller, a professor of religion, points out that "we worship the Gods and Goddesses one at a time, to be sure, but they are all at play in our culture and in our thinking and speaking about the deepest affairs of man in that culture."[1] Mythic images reflect our experience on a most profound and personal basis. Without courage and perspective, we run the risk of blindly accepting traditional images of dogmatic authority that hamper our connection with the Divine. By engaging an experience of the sacred, we become able to cast our own images - opening to the possibility of immersing ourselves in the numinous realm of God, the Gods, and the Divine in whatever tradition we practice.

Now more than ever before, it is time for humanity to reclaim a deeply personal experience of the Divine and to establish and sustain that communion. It is time for an experience beyond words, a love that casts out all fear, a joy that overshadows even our deepest despair, and a peace that surpasses rational understanding. Both East and West provide invitations to such an experience, as exemplified by the *Tao Te Ching* of China, the *Bhagavad Gita* of India, and the *Bible* and *Koran* of the West. Such texts are testaments to humanity's legacy of relating with the sacred.

Yet, do we have the presence of mind, the depth of reflection, to recognize the urgency of the invitation? Can we see the signs of devastation in our everyday worlds beckoning us to rededicate ourselves to wholeness? Can we put aside our self-seeking, self-gratifying urges for even a moment to enter the reality of a Divine Presence calling us forth?

The story of *Phaethon* comes to us from Greek and Roman mythology, yet the tale of pride leading to the fall can be found in all cultures - for the human spirit is characterized by the archetype of self-reflection, in spite of our efforts to relentlessly pursue the drives of the ego. Transcending thousands of years, the message in the tale of *Phaethon* still burns brightly – illuminating the pathos of our current moment. History has been an unfolding story - cycles of exodus from the slavery and domination of self-seeking urges to the empowerment of spiritual realization that emanates from our deep interrelation with the cosmos. This reciprocity delights in the underlying unity of all things and all beings while at the same time exalting the sublime beauty of diversity. Contrary to oft-held beliefs, our instinctual heritage is not a sign of "original sin." Instead, our heritage is actually one of deep, spiritual inquiry, with the relative freedom to follow where that inquiry leads. Our instincts are the energetic material to be reshaped and molded into character by all who are courageous and willing to hone and direct their energies toward life-affirming ends. The heroes of our moment are not explorers of the material worlds of science, commerce, and technology so much as courageous souls willing to immerse themselves in the depths of Spirit.

Ω

The treatment of the story of *Phaethon* that follows is divided into four chapters, each dealing with the different and deeper levels of perspective that this story reveals. These four levels of appreciation are the literal, the thoughtful, the heartfelt, and the spiritual, which appeal to and evoke response from the body, the mind, the heart, and the soul. Together, they reflect an ancient tradition that is known in the West as *Lectio Divina,* or Divine Reading, revealing the four senses of a sacred text. Each level opens up a new horizon of appreciation and presents a unique way of approaching the material. With the literal, we are allowed to experience *the facts* of the story through the sense of imagination. When we engage in thoughtful reflection, *the meaning* of the story begins to reveal itself. As we move to the level of the heartfelt, *a moral response* to the story emerges. The final level, the spiritual, opens up a well of infinite *value* that holds the power to heal and transform, to reveal soul.

Only as we move into the story in all four dimensions (literal, thoughtful, heartfelt, and spiritual) will we unveil the full measure of the gifts the story offers. In reality, our quest for meaning is a never-ending path to deeper and more profound perspectives. To remain on the surface of a literal interpretation of a sacred text is to miss the life-transforming meanings and values contained in sacred literature. *Phaethon* illustrates that the universe itself is a sacred text calling for a profound appreciation of its sublime values.

The story of *Phaethon* is particularly relevant today. As retold by Ovid, this myth is both a mirror of our human condition and a window into the promise and potential of our short but meaningful existence. As with all other sacred stories, the story of *Phaethon* offers meaning at a literal level, laying out the facts of devastation and of death that are the consequence of self-seeking folly. At an allegorical level, the story reveals deeper meaning by immersing us in the character of the human condition, its legacy of ancient, instinctual urges - raising the question of *original sin*. At a moral level, *Phaethon* calls for a heartfelt response of wise and compassionate action. And at the level of divine engagement, the story invites the reader to enter into an intimate, inward experience of divine relationship of healing and transformation, transcending words, and invoking contemplation and silence.

Phaethon invites us to appreciate our mythic moment by unveiling the powerful effects of our evolutionary urges upon the planet's landscape. As we survey that landscape, deep ecological sensitivities will be awakened because the devastation we are causing to the environment is quite real. A shift in consciousness is necessary. We enter the gate to an ordered cosmos with precise mathematical attributes and elegant universal truths, a garden of sublime beauty and exalted goodness. We discover in this sacred place an unfolding adventure filled with uncertainty, risk and divine opportunity. We become aware of our role in that cosmos as stewards and co-partners in the evolutionary panorama of the Earth. Visionaries such as Rachel Carson, Theodore Roszak, Annie Dillard, and Thomas Berry help us to see how our economic decisions have created trails of tears for every species upon the planet. The trails lead to our own front door. Writes Rachel Carson: "a child's world is fresh and new and beautiful, full of wonder and excitement. It is our misfortune that for most of us that clear-eyed vision, that true instinct for what is beautiful and awe-inspiring, is dimmed and even lost before we reach adulthood."[2]

Please allow the myth of *Phaethon*
to open your eyes,
your mind,
your heart and soul
to an indestructible sense of wonder.

Michelangelo Buonarroti (1475-1564)

ACKNOWLEDGMENTS

I thank Ovid for his rendition of the story of *Phaethon* and Allen Mandelbaum for his sensitive translation of Ovid's *Metamorphoses* for the world of the 21st century.

I thank Dr. Dana White for his invaluable service as the editor, designer, and producer of this book, and Michele Vercoutere for her eagle eye and proofreading.

I thank Dr. Raymond M. Alf, one of greatest of teachers and paleontologists to have left his footsteps on the sands of time, who taught me the awesomeness of our cosmos as well as the joys of the spiritual adventure.

To his understudy and bone-digging paleontologist, Dr. Don Lofgren, I also express my deep gratitude.

I thank the staff of Pacifica Graduate Institute near Santa Barbara, California, for their commitment to bringing a new awareness to our beleaguered planet, especially Drs. Dennis Patrick Slattery, Lionel Corbett and Rick Tarnas. Part of the enchantment of my work has been the privilege of working with a contemplative poet, an alchemical psychologist and a cosmic philosopher!

And, I thank every person who takes seriously the need for personal metamorphosis.

Although there are many translations of Ovid's *Metamorphoses*, our reference for this book is Allen Mandelbaum's translation of *Ovid's Metamorphoses*, published by Harcourt Brace & Company (1993), New York, London, and San Diego. I encourage you to purchase a copy for yourself and to plumb the depths of the book's ancient wisdom!

My soul would sing of metamorphosis!

Ovid

PHAETHON,
SON OF APOLLO

In many ways, the story of *Phaethon* is our story.

His presumptuous attitude is our attitude. His reckless journey is our journey. And unless we are able to learn from Phaethon, his tragedy will be ours. *Phaethon* is a particularly timely myth for us because it is a storyboard for the current human condition. The story reveals the destructive power of our inherited urges and the potential they have to undo the beauty and majesty of the planet's biosphere. *Phaethon* is a story that deserves both deep reflection and a legitimate response. The choice is ours whether we will avert a course that appears to be steering us toward greater destruction of the earth, the sky, the seas, and the planet's inhabitants.

The Story

Phaethon's story is a simple one - and although there are many variations and interpretations, the Ovid rendition is both clear, as translated by Allen Mandelbaum, and it hones the essence of a tale whose roots are deep in the oral tradition of human culture. Phaethon is the son of Apollo[⊕] — the Sun God, and Clymene - the ocean nymph. A confused son, neglected by his father, beloved and raised until adolescence by his mother, Phaethon confronts authority, searches for recognition, and in the process destroys himself and others. Phaethon is insecure — a fragile young man who

---

[⊕] Apollo is sometimes referred to by Ovid as Phoebus or Helios.

lacks guidance and perspective – not least from his father, Apollo, who is always too busy with his work that includes moving the sun about the heavens. Without guidance, Phaethon develops some bad habits and a false self-image. The myth portrays a young mortal (only his father Apollo is a god) who neither understands nor appreciates his divine heritage. Ovid writes, "when Jove fashioned man, his mold recalled the masters of all things, the gods." (8)

Phaethon allows his pride to motivate actions of excess that bring tragedy to him and the entire creation. It is a story that suggests not even nature is safe from the impetuous actions of humankind. In a world filled with ignorance and pride, Phaethon manifests that "audacious" spirit which Jove had sought to eradicate in the Greek version of the story of the flood.

Ovid writes:

Men live on plunder;
Guests cannot trust hosts…
Even brothers show scant love and faith…
This new race despised the gods…
When Jove, the son of Saturn, saw this scene
From his high citadel, he groaned… (8-10)

In the myth, Apollo drives the Sun across the sky each day in his magnificent chariot, the gift of Vulcan, driven by his four great steeds. Apollo is one of the many lustful deities of ancient Greece and Rome who would stop at nothing to fulfill their self-seeking licentious ambitions.

One can only imagine Apollo boasting to Clymene as he chased her through the fields, "consider who your lover is!" (23) It is easy to imagine that in such an environment that Phaethon was conceived in the flames of patriarchal domination, only to be raised by his mother, the subject of neglect by his father.

One day Phaethon boasts of his divine father, "so proud to have the Sun as father," (33) and is roundly taunted by one of his young friends, Epaphus, who says,

> Fool, do you think that all your mother says is true –
> Those lying tales that swelled your head? (33)

Phaethon runs to Clymene for confirmation of his claim to divine parentage. She tells Phaethon to visit his father in order to find out for himself. Clymene tells him,

> By all the radiance and light of one
> Who sees and hears us now, I swear, dear son,
> That you are born of this same Sun who stands before you
> As the world's great guardian. (34)

Phaethon is assured by his mother.

> He leaps with joy…
> He crosses his own Ethiopia;
> He passes India, the land that lies beneath the solar
> fires of the sky;
> And soon the boy has reached the very place
> From which his father rises, Phoebus'[⊕] palace. (34)

> The soaring palace of the Sun with all its giant columns,
> Was ablaze with gold and bronze, as if aflame;
> Its pediments were crowned on high with polished ivory;
> And glowing silver graced the double doors. (37)

⊕ Phoebus is Apollo.

Phaethon's heart leaps even higher as he encounters the splendor of his father's palace. The light is dazzling. Phaethon steps before Apollo:

> There, on a throne where fiery emeralds glowed,
> Sat Phoebus, in his regal purple cloak...
> There, flower-crowned, stood Spring;
> And naked Summer, wreathed with stalks of grain;
> And Autumn, stained with trodden grapes;
> And glacial Winter, with stiff white locks.
> There, with his eyes that oversee all things,
> The Sun, down from his towering throne,
> Could see his son bewildered by this strange new scene.
> He said: 'Dear Phaethon, what brought you here?
> What are you seeking in this fortress –
> Why come here, o son I never shall deny?'

The boy replied:

> "O you, the common light of this vast world,
> O Phoebus, who are my own father –
> If you say I have the right to use that word, and if it is no lie,
> A false guise that Clymene used to hide her shame –
> Remove my doubt, give me some proof,
> O Father, that I am your son in truth!" (38)

In an effort to comfort his estranged and neglected son, Phoebus embraces Phaethon. "I have no cause to say you are not mine; Clymene's words about your birth are true." (38) He then offers him the awesome, but fatal gift: "To set you free of any doubts, ask what you will of me: whatever gift you want, you shall receive." (38)

Without hesitation, Phaethon asks Apollo "to have his father's chariot – for one day, to guide its winged horses on their way" (38) in recognition of his status as Apollo's son. Phaethon's behavior is "launched in ignorance." (42) He is not willing to listen when he is told by his own father that "not even he who rules immense Olympus (Jove) can keep on course ... (Apollo's) chariot (39). Three and four times the god shook his bright head; repenting of his promise." (38) Apollo pleads with Phaethon to abandon his request, "the surest proof that I'm your father is my fear for you. Look at my face! And would you could inspect my heart and learn what cares a father bears! I implore you: make a wiser choice!" (40)

Phaethon is guided solely by his youth and inexperience: a pawn to his instincts for personal affirmation and self-gratification. He lacks maturity and the capacity for intelligent reflection, awareness of consequences, and consideration of others. Most of all, Phaethon lacks humility. Unable to harness his energies or bridle his passions, his youth is caught by the urge to prove his worth. If he could only realize how his impatience would produce calamity and devastation, surely he would not insist on taking Apollo's chariot across the sky. No rational person would compel the chaos and death that Phaethon brings as a result of his impetuousness. Even Apollo willingly admits to his own terror as he courses the sky each day in the chariot of fire: "my heart is rocked with terror and dismay as I see earth and sea far, far below. (39) What you now seek is not a blessing, but punishment. This request brings with it not...fame, but suffering. His warning now is done." (40)

Phaethon "resists his father's plea; the boy insists; he longs to guide the chariot. (40) Phaethon has leaped into the chariot: he takes his place with pride." (42)

Recognizing the folly of Phaethon, Apollo tries to provide some advice to his foolish son: "your only task will be to hold in check their racing feet...you cannot miss the tracks my wheels have left…don't ride too high, and do not sink too low: too high – and heaven's halls will burn; descend too low – and earth will meet its flaming end." (42)

And so Phaethon starts out across the morning sky, the dawn, "rejoicing" with an illusory sense of conscious control, experiencing a few, very few, ecstatic moments of elation and pleasure. Once Phaethon rises into the heavens, the four horses – Fire, Flame, Brilliant and Dawn – become aware that their true charioteer, Apollo, is not holding the reins. They immediately sense that whoever is holding the reins is a novice and not in control. The four steeds go "berserk – desert their customary course: no rule, no order governs their wild rush … he's lost control (43)." Unrestrained, they proceed according to their own passions paying no heed to the terrified lad in the chariot.

> But now the weight those horses bear is light;
> The pressure of the yoke is far more slight than
> they are used to.
> Lacking proper ballast, ships roll and rock
> among the waves – unbalanced:
> So did that chariot leap through the air,
> Tossing on high as if it had no rider.
> He does not know the horses' names […] (43).

The devastation of Phaethon's uncontrolled ecological disaster is captured well by Ovid with the destruction of the air:

> The clouds are scorched: they smoke […]
> Smoke runs from pole to pole!
> He cannot bear the torrid air he breathes…
> Thick smoke has shrouded him… (44, 45, 48)

with the destruction of the Earth:

32

The soil is drained of moisture; parched, it cracks;
The fields are blanched; the trees are ravaged,
stripped of green;
And, serving to efface itself,
Ripe grain provides the fuel that abets the blaze.
Yet these were but small griefs.
For greater still was the destruction of huge towns
and walls,
Whole regions and their peoples.
Woods and peaks catch flame: Mount Athos,
Taurus in Cilicia,
And Oete, Tmolus, and parched Ida
(once so rich with springs);
And Helicon, the slopes on which the virgin Muses
had their home... (44,45)

and, with the destruction of the seas:

The nymphs, their hair disheveled, mourned the loss
of springs and lakes [...]
Babylonian Euphrates also blazes...Ganges...
and the Danube ...
The Nile flees, terrified, out to the edges of the earth;
The sea shrinks...the dry sands spread ... the fish retreat
into the deepest seas,
And arching dolphins can no longer dare to leap –
as usual – into the air. (46,47)

As his father has predicted, Phaethon repents. But, sadly, it
is too late. Once Phaethon realizes that he has lost control   or was
never actually in control – the carnage and devastation burst forth
with abandon. In addition to the loss of his own life, Phaethon's
actions bring enormous devastation to the sky, the earth, the sea,
and all manner of habitation. As he is about to plummet to ashes,
Phaethon falls into depression, paralyzed:

Sad Phaethon looked down from heaven's heights at earth,
Which lay so far, so far below,
He paled, his knees were seized by sudden fright;
And there, within the overwhelming light,
A veil of darkness fell upon his eyes,
Would that he had never touched his father's steeds! –
So he repents. (43)
He's numb with fear…
He's stunned; frozen with fright,
He loses grip… (44)

The four horses of Apollo's chariot move without guidance.
"They follow random impulse; they collide with stars embedded in
the sky; they drag the reeling chariot on pathless tracts. Now they
rush upward; now they hurtle down…his team of horses sweep him
on – just as they please." (44,45) The devastation motivates Gaia,
the Great Mother Earth, to retreat into her deepest caverns. "And
mother Earth, around whom all the waters crowded close raised her
face – scorched her neck – and, wearily, at last lifted her hand up to
her brow and shuddered, shaking all things."(47)

In a powerfully moving plea, Gaia asks Jove to stop the
damage to herself and to her children.

Her words were stifled as she begged:
'Great Lord of all the gods,
If I indeed deserve this fate, and it's decreed,
Do not delay your thunderbolts!
For that would mitigate my ruin.
Even speech is hard for me – just opening my lips.
See, my hair is singed:
How many ashes blur my eyes, my face!
Is this how you repay me – the reward for my fertility,
My patient work? It's I who bear the harrow
and hooked plow;

Yearlong, I get no rest;
I furnish leaves to feed the beasts and harvests
for mankind,
Their peaceful food; and I, for you, provide incense.
But even if I've earned this end,
What suffering have the waters merited?
What has your brother Neptune done?
Why has the sea, the realm that fell to him by lot, shrunk so,
Retreating farther from the sky?
And if your brother's plight and mine do not move you,
Then pity your own heaven's fate.
Look here, look there: smoke runs from pole to pole!
If they should fall, your halls will also topple!
You see how even Atlas has to struggle:
He bears the white-hot axis on his shoulders –
But he is close to giving up.
If all three realms are ruined – sea and land and sky –
Then we shall be confounded in old Chaos.
Save from the flames what's left,
If anything can still be saved.
Think of the universe!
Here Earth fell silent…
And she withdrew into herself – into her deepest caves,
Recesses closest to the land of Shades. (47,48)

Hearing the cries of Gaia – Mother Earth – observing the
devastation of the earth, sky and seas, "the Almighty Father, calling
on the gods as witnesses, declares that if he does not intervene, all
things will face a dread catastrophe." (48)

He climbs to heaven's highest point,
The place from which he sends his cloud banks
down to earth,
From which he moves his thunder and deploys his bolts
of lightning…
After balancing a lightning bolt in his right hand,

From his ear's height he throws that shaft at Phaethon;
And it hurls him out of both his chariot and his life;
The god quells fire with savage fire! (48)

Phaethon falls from heaven, spiraling down to the earth, lifeless, a casualty of his own reckless abandon. "The waves of the Po (river in Italy) now bathe the boy's scorched face. There, in the west, the Naiads bury Phaethon's body, burned; upon his stone they carve these lines:

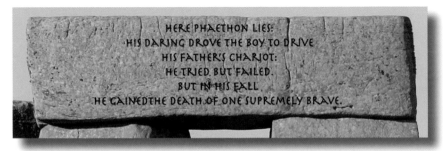

HERE PHAETHON LIES:
HIS DARING DROVE THE BOY TO DRIVE
HIS FATHER'S CHARIOT;
HE TRIED BUT FAILED,
BUT IN HIS FALL
HE GAINED THE DEATH OF ONE SUPREMELY BRAVE.

Perhaps this is the best epitaph for one so brazen and impetuous, so foolish and selfish. Clymene becomes hysterical when she learns of Phaethon's death.

She tore her robes; across the world she wandered,
Searching for his lifeless body at first, and then his bones;
And these she found at last along the foreign riverbank
Where they'd been buried.
Clymene lay prone upon that grave; her warm tears
Bathed the stone on which she read his name;
Beside the Po with her bared breasts,
She warmed his sepulcher. (49)

Phaethon's sisters, the Heliades, are demonstrative in their grief as well. As each of the sisters laments her brother's death, "bark enfolds their groins and, step by step, their bellies, their breasts, their

36

The Sisters of Phaethon
Santo di Tito (1536-1603)
Palazzo della Signoria
Florence, Italy

shoulders, then their hands; and all that's left uncovered are their mouths that call upon their mother."(50) Their tears transform to amber, launching cycles of metamorphosis and rebirth.

Then a cousin of Phaethon, Cycnus, "linked by deep affection," went to mourn the loss of his dear relative, "along the Po's green banks, where now the three sisters of Phaethon were new-made trees."(51)

"As he wept, his voice grew faint, his hair was hid beneath white plumage, and his neck grew longer, stretching outward from his chest…Cycnus had become a swan, who does not trust his wings to seek the sky of Jove, as if that bird recalled the cruel lightning bolt the god had hurled. And so the swan seeks out still pools and broad lakes; hating all that's fiery, he chooses water…"(51)

After the transformations of Phaethon's sisters and cousin, Jove inspects the heavens, the earth, and the seas. The heavens "have all held fast and kept the strength they had in ages past."(52) Of the earth, Jove "gives the soil its grass again; the trees, their leaves; the injured forests now grow green at his command."(52) Of the waters, "he restores the flow of springs and rivers: they resume their course."(52)

Thus ends the tragic tale of Phaethon. As we read the story, we cannot help but reflect upon a tale that so illuminates our own mythic moment. It beckons us to respond.

37

A REFLECTION ON THE STORY

PHAETHON, SON OF APOLLO

As we read the story of Phaethon, the pain of immense present-day damage to the earth, sky, and sea and their inhabitants caused by the self-referenced behaviors of humankind is apparent. From one continent to the next, no part of our habitat remains untouched. Ecologist Theodore Roszak writes, "the Earth's cry for rescue from the punishing weight of the industrial system we have created is our own cry for a scale and quality of life that will free each of us to become the complete person we were born to be."[3] Are the signs evidenced in our world today indicative of a deep yearning for wholeness within the human soul? Are the Earth's cries our own cries for help? Can we see that Phaethon's story reflects our own mortal predicament? Do we have the ability to avert the high-flying course of disaster upon which we find ourselves?

Marie-Louise von Franz, the close colleague of the great Swiss psychiatrist, C.G. Jung, shared Jung's deep concern about whether in view of humanity's rapid ascent in technology we could sustain our existence on the planet. In an interview, she refers to apocalyptic visions that Jung had near the end of his life. Von Franz indicates that she too had serious reservations about the future of humanity and life itself. "The beauty of all life, to think that billions and billions of years of evolution, the buildup of the plants and the animals and the whole beauty of nature, and to think that man would destroy it all out of sheer foolishness … that all life might go from the planet is so abominable." She adds, "Jung never thought we might do better than just sneak around the corner without not too big a catastrophe." In *Remembering Jung*, she describes Jung's visions as "enormous stretches devastated … enormous stretches of the earth. Thank God it is not the whole planet."

Ω

A Prologue of Pride

Ovid's story of *Phaethon* comes very early in the telling of the *Metamorphoses*. It is preceded by the stories of Io and Jove, Daphne and Apollo (Phoebus), Deucalion and Pyrrha, and the Greek version of the Flood myth.

Luigi Ademolli (1764-1849) produced engraved illustrations for one of the first printings of Ovid's Metamorphoses.

The stories of Io and Daphne are similar in that they reflect stories of abuse by the gods, and they are similar to the story of *Callisto*, which comes immediately after that of *Phaethon*. Neither Io nor the beautiful Daphne nor Callisto is interested in the sexual advances of the adulterous divinities, Jove and Apollo. These maidens enjoy their status as virgin warriors of Apollo's sister, Diana. In these stories, Jove and Apollo commit rape. Self-seeking, power-hungry and patriarchal, they neither woo nor seduce, but instead overpower their women – blind to the idea of love or respect for anyone else. These moments are opportunities to express power and control. In the case of the beautiful maiden Io, the abuse comes not only from Jove but also from Jove's wife, Juno. Juno's own emotional outburst of anger toward Io blinds Juno and does not allow her to reflect upon or differentiate between the abuser and the abused, which then contributes to further abuse.

"What misery!" cries out the father of Io, Inachus, a river god. One can feel the deep sense of despair and depression of Daphne's father, Peneus, as he consents to the metamorphosis of his precious daughter into the laurel tree in order to protect her from the lust of Apollo. The laurel becomes the beloved tree of Apollo and ironically, Apollo's legacy can still be recognized as the symbol of victory at the Olympic games.

Instead of seeing the laurel tree as a symbol of tragedy, it is important to see the tree as the revelation of nature's sacred power and numinosity, as well as its capacity to be a site of reconciliation and healing. Unlike the maidens pursued by the gods, nature eludes their grasp and ours. Myths convey the corridors of human interchange with the divine, especially through nature. Virtually every metamorphosis in Ovid carries the subject back through evolution, returning us to the womb of nature, as if nature, the

Great Mother, were the safe haven beyond the abusive tendencies of pride, whether human or divine. Ovid's answer to the abuse and destruction that has characterized human history is found within nature: the radiant laurel leaves of the nymph, Daphne, within the most lovely white heifer that is Io, within the amber tears of Phaethon's sisters, the Heliades, within the earthen face of Aglauros, within the beautiful yellow center circled by white petals of the Narcissus flower, and the beautiful white plumage of Cycnus, the swan of still waters.

Pride runs deeply through the stories of Io and Daphne. Apollo yells to Daphne as she flees him: "You don't know whom you're fleeing from. I am the lord of Delphi's land!" (23) "So Phoebus burns, so is his heart aflame; with hope he feeds a fruitless love." (22) Jove speaks boldly to Io, "I am He who holds within his hand the heaven's scepter: I am He who hurls the roaming thunderbolts. So do not flee!" (26) Blind, burning pride fills these stories. In the story of Callisto, we read, "a flame erupted in his (Jove's) bones." (53) Juno, Jove's jealous wife, is also the victim of her own pride. Ovid tells us that Juno "unleashed her rage," like a mad dog; "she drove the frightened girl (Io) across the world – a fugitive." (32)

Our self-seeking pride transforms others into objects and does not give ground for others to engage their own subjectivity, as if meaning and value were resident only in our ego. Our pride disenchants nature, strips nature of its intrinsic value, and transforms it into something to be used, exploited, and converted into material to serve our needs and wants. It turns the universe into a collection of objects, an "it," in such a way as to blind us to the life and soul of nature. This inevitably leads to tragedy and suffering because as nature vanishes, the best nature can hope for is to become a memory. Once a species is gone, it can never be recovered. We are left with the ashes, fossilized remains, and legends of nature. In the end, our objectification of nature's sacred character shuts us off from the light of heaven and our own redemption.

Nature mysteriously contains within her bosom – the rivers and seas, birds, beasts, and insects, flowers and fauna   an infinite array of alchemical interplay. Each part influences and shapes the whole – butterflies in one part of the earth motivating great chains of response in the reaches of faraway places. Nature reveals - if we can see – webs of interconnection and synchronicity, which convey much grander, more elegant fields of meaning and value than the rational capacities of our psyche apprehend. Ovid's stories flesh out the tragedy of humans caught in the webs of their arrogance, suggesting additional metamorphoses, each holding the capacity for numinous insight, anticipating further evolution, and continued transformation of consciousness as nature's evolutionary tale winds forward in time. Is a cycle of tragedy the fate and destiny of humankind? Or can we break from the pattern?

Deucalion, Pyrrha and the Flood

Ovid's stories of pride, lust, abuse and neglect stand in stark relief when contrasted to the story of the flood – of Deucalion, who was the Noah of the ancient Greek parable. As husband and wife, Deucalion and Pyrrha live humbly and charitably, their faith, hope and love abundant – worshiping God, tending the land, and honoring each other. Theirs is a simple existence, filled with a powerful "love for justice, … two beings who were pious, innocent." (15) They recognize the uncertainties that come with life on earth – dangers from nature as well as people. Still, they are committed to a higher set of values. Deucalion says to his Pyrrha, "if the sea had swallowed you, dear wife, I, too – believe me – would have followed you and let the deluge drown me, too."(17)

It is ironic that Deucalion becomes the sole male survivor of the devastating flood, because Deucalion is the son of Prometheus, the archetypal rebel who stole fire from the gods to give to humankind. Further complicating the drama, Apollo is the son of Jove. Prometheus is the mortal whom Jove arguably detests most, thus the wheels of redemption and rebirth turn full circle when Deucalion, great-grandson, is spared by Jove – even though Prometheus, the grandson, must endure 30,000 years chained to the rock. Aeschylus, the Greek poet, prophetically tells us it is the progeny of Prometheus and Deucalion, "the thirteenth generation," who will overthrow the old order of divinities and values and bring a new order.[4] Thus, the myth of *Prometheus* is indeed seminal. It is as if Jove foresees the day when his pantheon will not reign supreme, mindful that his patriarchy and archaic values will be replaced by an ethos of respect and inclusion. In Ovid's world, in spite of the deep uncertainties of mortal existence and the tragic appearance of suffering and chaos, there is indeed hope.

In Hesiod's account of the story of *Phaethon*, Phaethon is

 the son of the goddess Dawn (Eos or Aurora), and Hesiod's account has nothing to do with Apollo. Aurora symbolizes awareness of beginnings – the genesis of humanity as well as the dawn of each new day. Captured in frescoes and pottery by

artists often relegated to anonymity,
Aurora guides the chariot of the
sun from darkness into daylight.

In Hesiod's rendition,
Phaethon is seduced by his mother,
Eos. It is an incestuous relationship,
and Phaethon identifies with her
with terrifying results. The Hesiod
version of Phaethon suggests
that the unwillingness to move
courageously past our childhood
and transcend our childish urges represents a greater unwillingness
to allow emerging self-awareness to come forth, thus sacrificing
freedom and inviting disaster. Both versions point to the same end:
we must overcome pride and self-deception if we intend to avoid
the calamities that are the consequences of poor choice.

Much of our uneasiness can be understood by seeing how
our instinctual animal heritage, our childhood that we have yet to
transcend, is making it more difficult for us to perceive our divine
destiny. Whether we have lost faith or failed to ask the questions,
our eagerness to tap into the economic benefit of material existence
blinds us to the governing principles of nature and the cosmos. Like
Phaethon, we are convinced that we are ready to handle the reins
and are determined our time is now.

The tragedy in human history is that we are largely
unconscious of the motivation of our instincts and, all things
considered, we are still very much at the beginning of the story. In
order to move forward, we must transform self-seeking pride into
selfless compassion. In evolution, that which is unable to transform
or to adapt to new conditions perishes.

Fresco in Castle of Count Morra - Torino, Italy
Artist unknown

Die and be reborn.
Until you have learned this lesson,
You are but a dull guest
On a dark planet.

Goethe

AN EMERGING CONSCIOUSNESS

Apollo is a towering figure in both Greek and Roman mythology – one of the few gods to be spirited intact from the Greek pantheon to the Romans. He is a lynchpin in the study of mythological consciousness. The son of Zeus/Jupiter (Jove), Apollo is a warrior god whose mind and intellect are as sharp as his sword. Apollonian consciousness is characterized by analysis, self-reflection, and clarification – giving rise to the unfolding study of philosophy and culture. Paradoxically, Apollo courts the potential for self-destruction, for pride, and for narcissism. Thus, in the keystone above the portal at the temple of Apollo at Delphi in Greece (pictured right), we find the words *Know Thyself* etched in stone as an invitation to self-awareness.

Ovid's stories represent the emergence of a new stage of consciousness, with all its blessings and its residue of abusive destructiveness. He captured the myths at a time when the tidal wave of the written word was about to bury the oral tradition

47

beneath it. As images gave way to words in the mind, this
developing consciousness was accompanied by a heightened, albeit unformed and nascent, awareness of our individuality. This development may confuse a modern person because we view so much of our world through the scaffolding of language. It must be remembered that Ovid stood at the crossroads of two entirely different worlds of order – able to see both, and caught in the tension between the myths that were vanishing as stanchions

John William Waterhouse (1908)
Apollo and Daphne

supporting the pagan civilizations of ancient Greece and Rome and the cultures that would evolve into the Christian church.

Mythic consciousness is sometimes referred to as a condition of *participation mystique* that Jung describes as the most primitive level of awareness in which "individuals are still undifferentiated from each other, that is to say, they have not yet been self-consciously broken up into individual personalities."[5] The lack of differentiation extends further to include the natural world which is either inhabited or controlled by the gods and goddesses in an elaborate dynamic of divine interchange. The gods and goddesses are the most lingering evidence of humanity's mythic entanglement. We can only imagine today how deeply the deities of the natural world affected the people of ancient cultures. During most of our development from pre-history, humankind has been minimally self-conscious or self-reflective, and it must be considered that the myths – even if they seem filled with insight – were conceived and delivered from within the culture's deepest psychological waters.

In context, the myths, gods and goddesses were entirely oral. What we know of them today survives as the afterglow of a way of viewing the world long ago, covered by centuries of literary tradition. The gods voiced themselves through the myths of the culture, and people would not have seen themselves as separate from the story. In such a world, Jung tells us, "the ego has desperately little to say,"[6] which is one reason that he encourages the study of myth to understand our modern ego consciousness. Mythic consciousness exists in a state in which the fears of mysterious natural forces dominate and direct our behavior. The ego has yet to proclaim: "I am." Any sense of separation or individuality is still submersed in the consciousness of the collective whole. The primal appreciation of myth connects the present to the past, orienting the context, and pre-empting any need for the individual to ask, "whence, why and whither?"

Within the newly emerging consciousness in the stories of Ovid lies the potential of intelligent self-reflection and clarification, the advent of the scientific spirit as well as the promises of imagination. However, because it is so early in the development of rational consciousness, instinctual animal urges linger – reptilian and mammalian instincts that have been developed and refined over hundreds of millions of years of evolutionary history. These instincts and urges are invariably self-seeking in orientation because long before patterns, associations, and memory took hold in self-consciousness, the focus of attention was survival. The unwise expression of those urges that have motivated endless stories of tragedy in the pages of literature and recorded history, underwrites the behavior codes of civilized cultures, and is referred to in religion as our *original sin.*

It might be preferable to refer to these urges as our *original condition.* Jung describes the sharp edge of our emerging consciousness with an implicit allusion to mythic characters such as Phaethon, Icarus, and Bellerophon:

> This uprooted consciousness can no longer appeal to the authority of the primordial images; it has Promethean freedom, but it also suffers from godless hybris. It soars above the earth and above mankind, but the danger of its sudden collapse is there.[7]

The birthing of consciousness may have been a painful time for people and cultures alike – filled with atrocities and unimaginable suffering. It is both curse and blessing that there is sufficient awareness during the Classical era to recognize that the pain of coming into personal consciousness is accompanied by the first sparks of moral sensitivity, aesthetic appreciation, and notions of truth and justice. Aeschylus, Sophocles, and Euripides are among the literary bards and prophets of the Classical era. In *The Bacchae,* we see Euripides grappling with the possibility of a meaningful existence:

> Blessed is he who emerges from under affliction. Ten thousand men possess ten thousand hopes. A few bear fruit in happiness; the others go awry. But he who garners day by day the good of life, he is happiest. Blessed is he![8]

Nearly two millennia later, Thomas Hobbes, Bertrand Russell, and Arthur Schopenhauer would exalt tragedy as the final meaning of our existence, as the only genre in life's play. Hobbes

"Apollo and Daphne" fresco
Galleria Borghese - Rome, Italy

writes, it is "solitary, poor, nasty, brutish and short."[9] Russell tells us that "all the noonday brightness of human genius is destined to extinction."[10] He goes on to say, "brief and powerless is man's life; on him and all his race the slow, sure doom falls pitiless and dark."[11] Schopenhauer laments, "the life of every individual … is really *always* a tragedy."[12] Within the myth of Phaethon, the nagging question haunts us: is the life of the individual *always* a tragedy?

Comedy in drama and literature provides ample evidence that tragedy is not necessarily the end of the story. Comedy confronts the notion of inevitable tragedy, shifting the emphasis from the pathos of the individual to the meaning and value in life's circumstances. As consciousness emerged full-force, tragedy and comedy functioned as the interweaving of the mind's internal and external psychological orientations. "Comedy is about uncertainty and the willingness of the mind to dwell in it imaginatively. Comedy is the realm of faith, hope and love – those things that are essential."[13] Indeed, Aristotle's classic example of tragedy, Sophocles' *Oedipus Rex*, is not a single play but three plays that work together thematically, in which a meaningful conclusion to the life of Oedipus is revealed in *Oedipus at Collonus*. The self-seeking, instinctual powers of Oedipus' eyesight that induced him to commit murder and incest are transformed into the numinous vision of insight. For Oedipus, wisdom emerges and although he is now blind, he can at last see. This is the promise of comedy. Tragedy becomes the anvil upon which a meaningful life may be forged.

Jean-Antoine Theodore Giroust (1788)
Oedipus at Collonus

Then it came about as they were going along and talking,
That behold, there appeared a chariot of fire and horses of fire
That separated the two of them.
And Elijah went up by a whirlwind to heaven.

2 Kings: 2:11

THE IMAGES OF PHAETHON

Phaethon has been interpreted by artists since it was
first captured in story. The myth has been rendered
in sculpture, painting, and drama, providing us with multiple, but
consistent, interpretations of the devastation. When we allow these
images to enter the mysterious landscape of the soul, a new and
profound impulse is provoked – humility. Humility avails us to
the participatory nature of our involvement on the planet as one
species among a multitude of other species. Images of the Earth's
devastation awaken and call for a renewed communion with nature,
leading to a new cosmological appreciation of our place in time and
space.

The *Chariot of Fire* is the central archetypal image of the
story – and it is the focal point around which the myth's dramatic
action revolves. Just as our technology connects us today to the
earth and the sky, so the ancients conceived of a means to illustrate
their connection to the cosmos. Thus, the chariot becomes the
vehicle for Phaethon's ascent and demise. It conveys how we have
seemingly captured the powers that warm and nourish the universe.
In one of his last works, *Mankind and Mother Earth*, Arnold
Toynbee, the historian and friend of Carl Jung, writes:

Thus we now stand at a turning-point in the history of the biosphere and in the shorter history of one of its products and denizens, mankind. Man has been the first of Mother Earth's children to subdue life's mother and to wrest out of the hands of life's father, the Sun, the fearful force of solar power. Man has now let this power loose in the biosphere, naked and untempered, for the first time since the biosphere became habitable for life. Today we do not know whether Man is going to be willing or able to avoid bringing Phaethon's fate on himself and on his fellow living beings.[14]

In his 1983 article on Phaethon for *Spring: A Journal of Archetypal Psychology and Culture*, Mike Perlman writes:

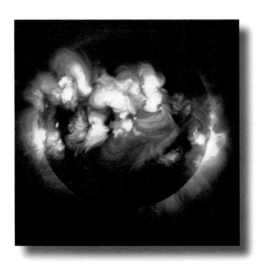

A thermonuclear explosion is essentially a small sun, and the effect of a sun in proximity to the earth is devastating. Phaethon, who brings the sun too close to earth, was himself imagined by the Greeks as 'a sort of younger or smaller sun.' Ovid, in keeping with this image, likens his fall to a shooting star. Phaethon's tragedy echoes that of other high-flying pueri such as Icarus and Bellerophon, but his nature is unique in its concentration of the solar or stellar aspect of puer consciousness.[15]

Phaethon serves as a metaphor of mortal identification with the sun, which the ancients took to be the source of life. Meeting the sun on its own terms, much less identifying oneself with the sun, and failing to show humility in the face of divine encounter courts blindness and devastation. Jung suggests that identifying oneself with an archetype constitutes the appropriation of the archetype to oneself – a project for which the mortal world is by nature unprepared. This represents our challenge – glimpsing the divine, developing the humility to stay in the shadow of divine influence, and resisting the urge and impulse to venture into the light to meet the divine as an equal. It is futile even to attempt to possess or control the divine. Our suffering is redeemed only by finding ourselves within the context of the archetype, being healed by the contact, and transformed by its numinous powers.

Jung cautions that we should, "never identify with an archetype … the consequences are terrifying."[16] Seeking to control the archetype of the chariot of fire stems from inflationary blindness. Only an ego devoid of self-reflection, a soul dimmed to the music of the divine spheres lacking the capacity to respect the gods would court such misadventure. This blindness and deafness is apparent in Phaethon when he refuses to listen to Apollo's heartfelt advice not to take control of the chariot's reins. French-Canadian psychologist Ginette Paris discusses the effects of identifying oneself too closely with the archetype of beauty:

> This exaggeration through an archetype always has disastrous results, no matter what the archetype is. The woman who 'thinks she's Aphrodite,' for example, makes people around her feel clumsy, lacking grace, as if she can never be given enough attention, approached with enough subtlety, whereas the true Aphrodisian personality radiates a charm that sheds a golden light to all those around and makes them appear their best. The former believes she is the mistress of a power, while the latter serves the archetypal power of Beauty and Attraction.[17]

Writing about Apollo, the archetype of intelligence, she says:

> The intellectual who 'takes himself for Apollo' doesn't
> realize at what point his sophisticated jargon becomes
> an obstacle to intellectual clarity. In his company, we feel
> suddenly stupid, we can't understand what he's talking
> about, we suspect his expert language isn't entirely justified
> by the complexity of the subject, and so we end up
> mistrusting intellectual reasoning as if it were a weapon
> to dominate others. He doesn't shed light on the subject,
> as a true Apollonian would do; he turns the spotlight on
> himself.[18]

She concludes her consideration of identifying oneself with the archetype by exclaiming: "Don't try to match a divinity, ever!"[19] Phaethon is a mortal brought to the face of a divine encounter. Yet, motivated by his ego need for self-gratification to harness the fiery energy of Apollo's horses, he scoffs at his father's graciousness, generosity, and repeated warnings. He is drawn "to match a divinity." Rather than taking up the inherited mantle to serve as a light-bringer, a humble co-partner with solar energy, Phaethon's ride in the chariot is about his own self-centered urge for power, control, and the compulsion to thrust the spotlight on himself. Of course, as we know this puerile maneuver results in terror and tragedy – scorching the lands, polluting the skies, and boiling the seas. He certainly did get noticed – with great devastation being the consequence. For Phaethon, childish pride truly fuels the chariot of fire into a tailspin.

In contrast to Phaethon, the prophet Elijah (opposite page) responded differently to God's still, small voice, and he was carried in a chariot of fire into the glory of heaven, there to be received joyously by the hosts of heaven.

The chariot of fire symbolizes the great possibility of the miracle of transformation – the eternal rebirth of time, nourishment, and light that stimulates growth. The chariot has been linked through the ages with the sun's significance as a source of light, heat, and energy, a fitting symbol for the material and spiritual nature of the divine. The charioteer symbolizes the possibility of transforming our instinctual urges so as to bring forth the opportunity of discovering new ways of being.

Elijah and the Chariot of Fire
Giuseppe Angeli (1712-1798)
National Gallery of Art - Washington DC

Phaeton Alarm'd
James Gillray (1757-1815)

Once, Phaethon – so proud to have the Sun as father – claimed
That he was better born than Epaphus,
Who met that claim with scorn:
"Fool, do you think that all your mother says is true –
Those lying tales that swelled your head?"

Ovid

CONTEMPORARY

PHAETHON

Edward Teller, the father of
the hydrogen bomb, was
fascinated by the thought of harnessing
the powers of the sun. "He was
gripped by the fascinosum, a numinous
image of unbounded fiery energy,"[20]
and a "fantasy of a thermonuclear
weapon of unlimited power."[21]
Arguably one of the brightest stars of
the twentieth- century's astronomical
age, Teller saw the power of the sun as
a way of controlling a perception of
fear. Rather than being motivated to

participate with the power of the sun, Teller seemed to manipulate
the fear behind the government's perceived need for greater power
and control to serve his own scientific ego ends: by developing a
weapon of incomprehensible explosive power to dominate others.

Teller spent his years after the Second World War advocating the nuclear arms race. During Ronald Reagan's tenure as President of the United States during the 1980s, Teller continued his fantasy of nuclear weapons domination by helping to inspire the dream of being able to ward off nuclear attack by use of

SDI technology, the so-called Star Wars defense.

We are told that Teller's "imagination, even at an early age, engulfed the cosmos."[22]   Like Phaethon, Edward Teller experienced a distant, often difficult relationship with his father. Teller reflected, "I was never able to talk to him easily; nor he to me."[23]   Teller describes his relationship with his mother that in many ways resembled Phaethon's relationship to Clymene. "My mother doted on me, and made no effort to hide her feeling."[24] As a youth, he "found the taunts of his schoolmates intolerable."[25] As if cast in the mold of Phaethon, Teller was characterized as having "a large and surprisingly fragile ego" with a "restless seemingly driven energy."[26] Almost prophetically, he writes about one of his most powerful early childhood memories: "My father gave me a little mirror and showed me how to reflect a sunbeam onto the ceiling. I was fascinated; I played with the mirror and sunbeams for hours."[27]

Edward Teller became "one of the most imaginative, creative physicists alive,"[28] yet he also could be impatient and extremely uncooperative. Rather than seeing himself as a man among men, Teller's imagination was driven by a deep compulsion to identify himself with and control the powers of the sun. Like playing with the sunbeams upon his ceiling as a child, his reach soon exceeded his grasp and rather than serve those powers humbly, he sought to bottle the sun's force and energy.

He often referred to the hydrogen bomb lovingly as "my baby."[29] It is said that he often exhibited "autocratic behavior and temperamental outbursts."[30] He and others desired to bend nuclear power to serve the human ego's fantasy of ultimate power and supreme control. Thus, like Phaethon, he too leaped into the chariot of the sun's power.

Twentieth-century physics seemed possessed by the possibilities of extending the limits of cosmological perspective. It became important to update both our understanding and the prevailing images of the heavens. Inevitably, however, as understanding of the cosmos shifts, we are compelled to revisit and re-vision our divinities. This, we know from the tribulations of Copernicus, Galileo, and others, is a social contract that is not easily brokered.

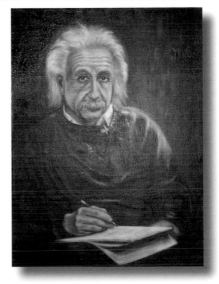

New values are birthed into people and cultures with great difficulty. Change may be written into nature's DNA – but humans seem peculiarly resistant to metamorphosis. Albert Einstein once mused, "I want to know how God created this world ... I want to know his thoughts, the rest are details."[31] Many of the early twentieth-century physicists, such as Einstein, Neils Bohr, and Werner Heisenberg, were moved by a quest to see the truth and the beauty of an ordered cosmos, a truth they discovered in the elegant logic of their mathematical pictures. Heisenberg remarked, "what something means is what it means in mathematics."[32] Like the classical mathematician-philosopher Pythagoras, Einstein, Bohr, and Heisenberg discovered an inherent magic, uncertainty, and beauty in the relationships of those mathematical pictures: a glorious mural of cosmos.

They discovered a physics of deep truth embedded in the many dimensions of an often paradoxical universe. They saw the elegance of emergence, diversity, and complementary relations in fractals, particles, and waves. They underscored the pivotal position of the human observer and the effect of observation upon nature by sustaining a reach into the realms of the natural world that was within their grasp – even as their reach extended as the frontiers of science moved outward. Yet with increasing discoveries came an awareness of our mortal limitations and the risks being courted – some technological, some philosophical, and some spiritual. While others persisted in seeking to elevate themselves above nature, in defying the limits of the physical and spiritual worlds, many scientists saw wisdom in cultivating deep humility. Einstein expressed the sincerity of his humility when he wrote:

> My religion consists of a humble admiration of the Illimitable Superior Spirit who reveals himself in the slight details we are able to perceive with our frail and feeble minds.[33]

This attitude toward reality led many of these early physicists to be humble and respectful as they poked and probed the universe.

They knew it would be childish and dangerous to think themselves equal or superior to the powers of the universe. Though Einstein did not fully subscribe to the God images cast by the *Torah*, he did believe the universe to operate as if governed by an autonomous power of superior intelligence. Again, Einstein writes:

> The human mind is not capable of grasping the Universe. We are like a little child entering a huge library. The walls are covered to the ceilings with books in many different tongues. The child knows that someone must have written these books. It does not know who or how. It does not understand the languages in which they are written. But the child notes a definite plan in the arrangement of the books ... a mysterious order which it does not comprehend, but only dimly suspects.[34]

Speaking about Edward Teller's work with the hydrogen bomb, Einstein warned: "If the (bomb) is successful, radioactive poisoning of the atmosphere and hence annihilation of any life on earth has been brought within the range of technical possibilities."[35]

Nagasaki, Japan - August 9, 1945

As if following the script of *Phaethon*, Teller responded:

> No one will be glad to discover more fuel with which a
> coming conflagration may be fed. But scientists must find
> a modest way of looking into an uncertain future. The
> scientist is not responsible for the laws of nature. It is his
> job to find out how these laws can serve the human will.[36]

This statement is reminiscent of that made by Francis Bacon, the philosophic progenitor of modern science and the inspiration of the Enlightenment, who declared that

> We must put nature on the rack and compel her to bear
> witness even against herself, so that we may control her to
> our ends - everything is possible to man. Time is young: give
> us some little centuries, and we shall control and remake all
> things. We shall perhaps at last learn the noblest lesson of
> all, that man must not fight man, but make war only on the
> obstacles that nature offers to the triumph of man.[37]

Teller exclaimed, "I consider it a certainty that the superbomb (the hydrogen bomb) will allow us to extend our power over natural phenomena far beyond anything we can at present imagine."[38] In a letter to fellow physicist Hans Bethe, Teller wrote that "physicists have known power,"[39] in reference to his close associate and one of the lead scientists in the development of the atomic bomb, Robert Oppenheimer, who confessed his regret that "physicists have known sin."[40] To the end of his life, Oppenheimer was disconsolate over the use of the power that he and his associates had sought to manipulate. Clearly troubled, he wrote to a friend around the time of the devastation of Hiroshima and Nagasaki that his feelings about the future were "only a stone's throw from despair."[41]

After Arjuna had spoken, Krishna drove the splendid chariot
And brought it to a halt midway between the two armies.
Arjuna saw them standing there:
Fathers, grandfathers, teachers,
Uncles, brothers, sons, grandsons, and friends,
Kinsmen on both sides, each side arrayed against the other.
Arjuna sank down into the chariot, his mind heavy with grief.[42]

Bhagavad Gita

SOLAR POWER,
A PERSPECTIVE
FROM THE EAST

On the white sands of Alamagordo, New Mexico, on July 16, 1945, Robert Oppenheimer responded to the blinding light of the first atomic explosion by reciting a verse from the epic Indian story, the *Bhagavad Gita*, an apocalyptic tale of depression and enlightenment, of war and of lasting peace.

> If a thousand suns were to rise
> And stand in the noon sky, blazing,
> Such brilliance would be like the fierce
> Brilliance of that mighty Self.[43]

Pre-empting the possibility of his own spontaneity, Oppenheimer came to the test site on that fateful morning prepared with a quotation that would advance a perspective that would compel reflection at the time, or perhaps thoughtfulness in the future. Did Oppenheimer have second thoughts now that his years of work on the atomic bomb were reaching catharsis? As the bomb exploded, Oppenheimer would offer yet another verse from the *Bhagavad Gita*: "I am death, shatterer of worlds, annihilating all things."[44] By the time the atomic explosion lit up the desert floor

in New Mexico, Teller had already segued his interests to an even greater power: the creation of the hydrogen bomb. This bomb would dwarf the explosive capacity of the atomic bomb that scorched the New Mexico sands that summer morning -- a bomb thousands of times greater in destructive capacity that would obliterate the world as we know it, forever. Stephen Mitchell, who has given us a recent translation of the *Bhagavad Gita*, asks: "What other image from world literature could have been so uncannily right for that occasion?"[45]

The most striking difference between the *Bhagavad Gita* and *Phaethon* is that in the *Bhagavad Gita*, when Krishna reveals his solar nature to Arjuna, Arjuna humbly submits and in that very moment is healed and transformed by the four disciplines of yoga: the yogas of wisdom (the mind), devotion (the heart), service (the body), and meditation (the soul).

As a warrior, Arjuna could not perform heroically in battle because of depression, a sense of his mortal limitations, and by sympathy for his family, many of whom had taken up battle against him and his brothers. Krishna infuses Arjuna with the power of wisdom to fight on the field of duty. He reveals a numinous, healing power for Arjuna to use in conflict – infused through humility and deep involvement in yogic metamorphosis. Krishna introduces Arjuna into a radically new mode of being in the world, drawing upon what Jung considers the four basic functions of the psyche: thinking, feeling, sensation and intuition. Arjuna becomes quiet and motionless, and in the silence and stillness, he discovers an inner voice of wisdom ennobling his warrior stance.

Facing Apollo in the myth of *Phaethon*, Phaethon is both confused and arrogant – wrong to assume that his boastful demeanor masks his incompetence and lack of preparation. He has convinced himself that he can control the power of the sun and no amount of appeal or concern from Apollo can dissuade him. Unwilling to listen to divine counsel, he will not back down. We see (captured on the ancient Greek vase below) that Phaethon's confidence is inflated with the heightened fantasy to prove his mettle and to demonstrate his prowess.

Phaethon's arrogance and conceit contrast sharply to Arjuna's deference and humility, and accordingly determines the quality of relations to the archetype. With humility, the moment of engagement becomes an opportunity for the self to perform – demonstrating techniques and prowess honed through experience. Arjuna went a major step further. Mindful of his own strengths and acumen, he recognized his dependence upon the powers of the universe and experienced from whence the powers emanate. Phaethon insisted upon controlling those powers, and he saw the forces as something external to himself and over which he sought dominion. Since his quest was to make the chariot a symbol of his own independence, taking control of the chariot and horses became fundamental to his self-expression. Arjuna knew with every fiber of his being that he existed in intimate and inescapable relations with the powers. While Arjuna submitted himself reverently before the archetype's divine power – being healed and transformed as a result, Phaethon sought to bend the power of the archetype to his own self-serving ends.

Both Arjuna and Phaethon heard the call for submission to the archetype. A comparison of the two myths makes it clear which provides the warrior with grace under fire.

Go over and over your beads,
Paint weird designs on your forehead,
Wear your hair matted, long, and ostentatious,
But when deep inside you there is a loaded gun,
How can you have God?

Kabir

THE SOLAR THREAT

In the more than sixty years since the first explosion of an atomic bomb, it is unclear exactly how many times we have come close to a nuclear holocaust. We know that we came close on three specific occasions, and probably more than that, during the Cold War. We also know that our best attempts to work

with nuclear power even for peaceful purposes have been beset by technological and operational problems. Speaking to an Israeli lobbyist in 1983, President Ronald Reagan confided:

> I turn back to your ancient prophets in the Old Testament and the signs foretelling Armageddon, and I find myself wondering if we're the generation that's going to see that come about.[46]

President Ronald Reagan with Israeli President Chaim Herzog, outside the Oval Office, 1987.

It is not a coincidence that in the same year depth psychologist James Hillman pulled together a conference of leading thinkers entitled *Facing Apocalypse*, at which he stated:

> Imagination seems ... to be the only safe place to keep the bomb. Mars wants more than reflection. Mars demands penetration toward essence, pushing forward ever further into the tangle of danger, and danger now lies in the unthought thicket of our numbed minds. Swords must be beaten into plowshares, hammered, twisted, wrought.[47]

In the fall of 1983, the United States had warships positioned off the shores of the eastern Mediterranean and North Korea on a state of high alert. Reagan's rhetoric against the evil empire of Russia caused many to speculate about the possibility of a real apocalypse. The lines of confrontation had been drawn and the global theater stood in a condition of readiness for war. Adding

to the political fervor of the Cold War, Christian fundamentalists such as Hal Lindsey were stirring up the waters with their polemical tomes. Lindsey's *The Late Great Planet Earth* sold twenty million copies – nearly one for every ten Americans at the time – offered a virtual recipe of the ingredients for a catastrophic self-fulfilling prophecy. Less impassioned, but no less concerned, philosophers and psychologists like Marie-Louise von Franz characterized the frenzy as "sheer shadow foolishness."[48] The 1980s were indeed conflicted times.

Amidst much celebration on both sides, in 1989 the Berlin wall that had truncated Germany came down. Although George H.W. Bush was the President of the United States at the time, the event has been appreciated as one of the hallmarks of Ronald Reagan's presidential legacy. A section of the colorful wall was transported to the Reagan Presidential Library in Simi Valley, California (shown opposite page).

With international concern still brewing, that same year Gordon Brook-Shepherd penned a startling book, *The Storm Birds: Soviet Post-War Defectors*, in which he quotes a well placed Russian authority describing the Russian plan during the tenure of Andropov to launch a preemptive nuclear strike upon the United States in response to what the Russians perceived as an eminent attack by NATO forces.

> When Gordievski, former KGB agent, was finally plucked from Moscow, he had given Britain and her allies a priceless flow of information as well as a chilling example of how paranoia in the Kremlin almost brought the world to war in the autumn of 1983... The incredible seemed to be happening, namely, that the Warsaw Pact suspected it might really be facing nuclear attack at any moment. What the West ... was totally unaware of at the time was how far it had really passed through a war danger zone in those early November days of 1983.[49]

When we look back to the beginning of the 1980s, we see that the puer consciousness of the world's leaders – both East and West – was on track to the skyward path of Phaethon. Their "adolescent psychology" manifest what Marie-Louise von Franz describes as a "pathological megalomania,"[50] one parallel to Phaethon's attitude and behavior.

Similar crises had been narrowly averted during the 1962 Cuban missile crisis and in 1979, when a technician in Omaha accidentally loaded a simulated attack scenario into our national defense warning system. In both cases, a nuclear holocaust was narrowly averted. Toward the end of his life in 1961, Jung had visions of vast stretches of devastation that were clearly anchored in his own immersion in, and sensitivity to, real-life events influencing the character of the collective soul of the world, the *anima mundi*.

> And now, as Jove was just about to hurl
> his thunderbolts at the whole earth,
> He stayed his hand:
> He was afraid that all those flames might
> set the sacred sky ablaze,
> Ignite the world from pole to pole.[51]

Einstein's premonition that thermonuclear devices hold the capacity to annihilate life on earth illustrates the proximity of our technological pride to imminent disaster. Life today is a heartbeat away from being extinguished by hubris, miscalculation, or simply bad judgment. In his last State of the Union address shortly before leaving office in 1953, President Harry Truman stated:

> The war of the future would be one in which man could extinguish millions of lives at one blow, demolish the great cities of the world, wipe out the cultural achievements of the past – and destroy the very structure of a civilization that has been slowly and painfully built up through hundreds of generations. Such a war is not a possible policy for rational men.[52]

Given our history and the uncertainties of our current times, two questions predominate:

1. How rational are we as a species?
2. Is rationality sufficient to address and deal with the present predicament?

The story of Thomas Aquinas, the Medieval scholastic whose theological work provides much of the rational foundation for the Catholic perspective, is illuminating with respect to the second of the two above questions. Thomas wrote what he called the *Summa Theologiae*, the Summary of Theological Thought, in which he addresses almost every conceivable philosophical and theological question, including proofs for the very existence of God. It is said that later in his life, while celebrating Mass, he fell into a swoon - having a numinous and mystical experience of great depth. He informed one of his colleagues after this experience that "all my work seems mere straw," the result of his encounter with the limits of his own rational approach to reality. The story imparts the necessity of integrating all of the psychic functions - including reason.

St. Thomas Aquinas
Sacristy of San Esteban
Salamanca, Italy

Cosmè Tura (Ferrare, 1430-1495)
Saint Antoine de Padoue lisant
Louvre - Paris, France

The truly great one
    Dwells on what is real,
        Not on what is on the surface.

Lao Tzu

THE RATIONAL HUMAN

For much of human history, the individuality that we in
the West consider tantamount to being "human" has
evolved and transformed. For aeons, hunting and gathering cultures
coexisted with nature – some peoples settled into communities
while others continued a nomadic existence. Then curiously
during the Axial Age (800 B.C.E. to 200 B.C.E.), in several different
cultures scattered across the planet, "individuality" took a giant
leap forward. As if the archetype of the Self were penetrating the
physics of the collective unconscious, within a relatively few years
in civilizations separated by vast oceans and continents, Buddha,
Lao Tzu, and Confucius in Asia, and Pythagoras, Plato, and Aristotle
in Greece began to explore and express the frontiers of personal
consciousness. The human psyche changed dramatically – forever!

Individuality today is very different from individuality in
ancient times. In fact, our sense of self today is dramatically different
than it was even fifty years ago. Moreover, individuality is unique
depending which country – and even which part of a particular
country – a person happens to call home. How a person arrives
at life-informing, value-producing conclusions is to a large extent
based upon how individuality factors into the broader collective
construct of nature and culture. For example, the "I" that is central

to the English-speaking world is really not the same "I" as in other languages. In English, we may say that, "I am cold or sad" – using the ego's experience of the weather and emotions as the reckoning point. Other languages, however, formulate the same idea by postulating the equivalent of "to me there is coldness or sadness," suggesting that conditions exist in and of themselves and are not directly referenced to the ego of the person. Accordingly, language can be seen as a sort of "text" that inscribes but also extends the boundaries, frontiers, and limits of our self-awareness. Individually and culturally, we have many texts that influence our ways of being – and the idea of text is evidenced most obviously in our language: contexts, subtexts, textures, and so forth. Applied to the psyche and the human experience, text carries profound implications that affect and define our personal and cultural circumstances. Yet our species continually dares to ask the question, who is this "I" that is speaking? And when it comes to our human faculties of reason, the differences are equally profound.

Reason represents the act of recognizing the frames of reference as well as the deductions that consciousness develops with respect to its own experience. Reason flows out of the text of our language and is prefigured by its relation to the facts, meanings and values of experience. These relationships articulate our worldview – making the world sensible from within a particular culture. In addition, reason is shaped by how we conceive the idea of individuality and by how we frame individuality within the context of psychological and cultural references. It is little wonder that, following the differences in contextualizing perspectives, there is immense variation among the world's civilizations regarding how the human and natural worlds coexist.

As we collectively move further into the new millennium –

with the immediacy of the Internet and the capability of feeling up close and personal with the most remote regions of the earth – it is becoming increasingly evident that the Western idea of individuality is influencing the psychology of people and cultures worldwide. Understandably, this influence is being perceived as a threat to some cultures' ways of life.

The proliferation of nuclear capability, particularly weapons, around the planet has brought humanity to the brink of potential demise. As long as the stockpiles of nuclear waste and active material endure, so long as war is regarded as a viable means to deal with political conflict, human existence will remain tenuous and uncertain. Until as recently as the middle of the twentieth century, the prospect of global annihilation had been a fantasy, for even the worst threat could be localized. Now, however, a global catastrophe is completely within the realm of possibility, and new potentials for extinction continue to emerge since the detonation of a nuclear device could take place anywhere in the world and would likely have a cataclysmic effect upon the entire planet – affecting both humans and the environment for centuries, if not forever. Paleontologists believe that what brought about the end of the age of dinosaurs sixty-five million years ago was a lone not-so-large meteor colliding with the earth somewhere near the Yucatan Peninsula. The consensus is that a nuclear event could dramatically eclipse the collision force power of a meteor.

It serves to ask, have our perspectives and our worldview matured at the same rate as our technological prowess? No one disputes our engineering and scientific achievements – building bridges and tall buildings, developing new materials, creating new medicines, and exploring new ways to process information, images, and sounds. These have become the symbols of material success

– and humans take great pride in celebrating control of this brave new world. Yet for all the horizons we have crossed, it seems we have not adjusted our psychology either to find the joy in the ride or to experience fulfillment. To be sure, if we do have a destination, our relentless pursuits of momentum and development – often for selfish ends – counter our best possible intentions, for like Phaethon we have little evidence we have mastered the forces propelling the human journey. Possessed by fear, greed, and a host of other passions, we remain trapped in the same vicious cycles as the ancients – demonstrating that the myths truly have an eternal nature about them.

During his tenure as President, Ronald Reagan once asked an audience to imagine that "all of us discovered that we were threatened by a power from outer space – from another planet." He then asked, "Wouldn't we come together to fight that particular threat?" After letting the image sink in, Reagan moved to the point: "We now have a weapon that can destroy the world – why don't we recognize that threat more clearly and then come together with one aim in mind: How safely, sanely, and quickly can we rid the world of this threat to our civilization and our existence?"[53]

So 'audacious' Phaethon looked down from heaven's
heights at earth which lay so far, so far below.
He paled, his knees were seized by sudden fright;
And there, within the overwhelming light,
A veil of darkness fell upon his eyes,
Would that he had never touched his father's steeds! –
So he repents.

Ovid

OUR PRECARIOUS CHARIOT

It is virtually impossible to read Ovid's story of *Phaethon*
without seeing the parallels to the current condition of
our world and without feeling deep sadness and remorse. Rooted
in ego and the seductions of reason and glorification of the self,
our Western cultural value systems and mythologies are carrying
us into a story that reads like the script of *Phaethon*. There is deep
discontinuity between the human species and the rest of creation
– evidenced by the number of species endangered or extinct,
the damage brought to the earth by human habitation, and our
failure to embrace our charter as the protector. This discontinuity
is further reflected by the lack of an adequate cosmological
perspective and the absence of an orienting metaphor to provide
spiritual insight. Simply put, there is precious little in the image- or
word-based architectures of thought that articulates a perspective
that will heal the rift between people and the natural world. People
have lost their connection to nature and to the cosmos. Churches
are being abandoned while the shopping malls are overflowing,
altars replaced by inventory shelves. The sacred has been silenced so
the secular can be heard. We have appropriated meaning and value
to all things human – inflating the value of the subjectivity of our

humanity, proclaiming that the world exists solely for our pleasure and self-gratification. Our attempt to realize Self in an instant without reference to the rest of life carries great peril.

The Roots of Division

Once self-consciousness took hold in the individual, the alienation of the individual from both the collective and nature became one of the consequences. Then, as now, believing in one's own capabilities and strengths built confidence and a base upon which to construct a foundation for continued development. It is, however, all too tempting to become infatuated with our accomplishments, skills, and self-image. The ancients recognized this, and with the stories of *Narcissus* and *Phaethon*, they cautioned against excessive self-reference. Today's world is beset by serious cultivation of hubris – both at the personal and collective levels, as much causing as a byproduct of alienation – a disconnection that fosters distrust of the "other" and glorification of the self, or ego.

From the time that Rene Descartes, the father of modern rationalism, conceived "Cogito, ergo sum," or "I think, therefore I am," the project of individualized consciousness has progressed steadily away from connection with everything to connection with nothing. The twentieth

Rene Descartes
Sebastien Bourdon (1616-1671)
Louvre - Paris, France

century may have begun with Sartre, Heidegger, and Camus proclaiming the ego's existential solidarity, but it culminated in a web of post-modern relativism – the utter subjectivity of language-based truths characterized by Foucault, Derrida, and waves of deconstructionists. We have de-constructed, de-centered, and dis-enchanted every nook and cranny of "reality." It seems that we now find ourselves in much the same condition as we were thousands of years ago – implicated in the infinite web of the cosmos. However, now we are inescapably and profoundly aware of it – and where the ancients had their myths to shelter, orient, and collectivize themselves, we live in the disheartening absence of a functional myth.

Great purpose is served by making sense of our connection to the numinous powers of divinity, which is affirmed in the West by the stories of the *Tanakh*, the *Gospels*, and the *Koran*. All too often, however, that connection does little to make sense of our relationship to the physical dimensions of the world, which are challenged as much today as at any time in history. However, when connection with the divine becomes confused, is severed or is cast aside, people can feel adrift or marginalized. They may resort to quick-fix or pseudo-indigenous spiritualities. In the end, visualizing humanity as the jewel in the crown of creation

Image of Indra's Net

costs us our intimacy and communion with the earth because our sense of being special or superior comes at a price. What is required is the image of Indra's net (see Page 81), wherein jewels are seen in every direction, clustered and interconnected as if woven into the miracle of *inter-being*.

We can no more transcend our earthly limits than Phaethon could master the chariot of Apollo. Both the desire and the fiction of rising up above our human limits rupture our coherence with the rest of mortal existence. Yet failing to see or accept the nature of existence, we, like Phaethon, scurry about the globe as if our actions are empty of consequence, believing that we have the ability and power to fix any problems we create. Filling the earth's skies with smoke and pollution from the North to the South Pole, humans have poisoned the earth's life-giving waters and stripped her fertile soil of minerals and nutrients. The sky above and the earth below have been injured by human contact. We even threaten the earth's ability to rejuvenate. Perhaps we are already immersed in an apocalyptic event, contributing to Jung's vision of the devastation of enormous stretches of earth, a devastation of both biological and imaginative resources. Perhaps global warming is the precursor of that devastation.

Jove had his own premonition:

He brought to mind that,
In the book of the fates, this was inscribed:
A time would come when sea and land would burn,

A conflagration that would overturn the palace of the sky –
In fact destroying the stunning fabric of the universe. (13)

Does such a premonition anticipate the supernova of our
sun five billion years from now, or might it reflect humanity's tragic
capacity for self-destruction?

Theodore Roszak writes:

> The ecological crisis of our time is either another detour
> along the open highway of economic progress, or it is the
> warning of a dead end just around the corner, a disaster
> far worse than the Black Death, from which it may take
> millennia to recover.[54]

Dr. Gerald O. Barney, director of the Millennium Institute,
compiled data relevant to the current level of devastation as well as
the projected trajectory in *Global 2000 Revisited*:

> As we look around us today, the struggle for life seems all the
> more perilous. Over the whole Earth, the human community
> and much of the entire community of life are now in serious
> danger. Most ominously, all of the biogeochemical systems
> essential for life on Earth, the habitats essential for the survival
> of diverse species, and even the atmosphere and the oceans
> are now disturbed and threatened on a planetary scale.[55]

Barney provides immense support and an array of alarming
statistics that should cause any normal person to look twice and
consider whether we do in fact have a legitimate environmental
crisis on our hands, and whether our current political and economic
ideologies should not shoulder the brunt of the responsibility. So,
let us ask, as we proceed into the twenty-first century, where do we
think we are headed and will we get there? Barney notes,

When thinking about the future and human needs in the future, it is necessary to consider the number of humans whose needs must be met. During the lifetime of adults today, human numbers approximately doubled from about 2.5 billion to about 5 billion. A key aspect of caring for the children of the future is food.[56]

Using graphs and statistics, Barney shows all of the potentially arable land in relation to the increase in human population, factoring in the effect of "arable land that is being lost through erosion, deforestation, expanding urban areas, depletion of irrigation water, salinization, water logging, and other factors."[57] The data demonstrate that we are on a collision course with our resource limits and that the capacity of the environment to respond will increasingly have more devastating effects planet-wide.

In *The Future of Life*, the Harvard biologist Edward O. Wilson provides yet another graphic illustration of our reckless journey:

The ecological footprint – the average amount of productive land and shallow sea appropriated by each person in bits and pieces from around the world for food, water, housing, energy, transportation, commerce, and waste absorption – is about one hectare (2.5 acres) in developing nations but about 9.6 hectares (24 acres) in the United States.

For every person in the world to reach present U.S. levels of consumption with existing technology would require four more planet Earths. Homo sapiens have become a geophysical force, the first species in the history of the planet to attain that dubious distinction. We have driven atmospheric carbon dioxide to the highest levels in at least two hundred thousand years, unbalanced the nitrogen cycle, and contributed to a global warming that will ultimately be bad news everywhere.[58]

Among the many alarming indicators that Gerald Barney has unearthed as critical to be addressed in the twenty-first century is the extent of the biocide that we are committing upon the creatures that live within, among, and around humanity on the planet. "By early in the twenty-first century, species will be vanishing forever at a rate of hundreds per day."[59]

Recently, the American Museum of Natural History in New York City posted on its website a press release stating:

1) We are in the midst of a mass extinction of living things. This dramatic loss of species poses a major threat to human existence in the next century,

2) The general public is relatively unaware of the loss of species and the threat that it poses,

3) This mass extinction is the fastest in Earth's 4.5 billion-year history and, unlike prior extinctions, is mainly the result of human activity.[60]

The major shifts in geologic time from the Paleozoic to the Mesozoic and from the Mesozoic to the Cenozoic were marked by mass extinctions. The current mass extinction engendered primarily by human

activity has led some cosmologists such as Brian Swimme and Thomas Berry to suggest that, once again, the earth is in the midst of another major planetary shift: the birth of a new aeon – the Ecozoic.

Because our cosmological stories are inadequate to the task of identifying the paths we should take to sustain the well-being of the planet, and because our mythic self-concepts embolden us to perpetrate continued devastation upon the planet, the stage is set for a conflagration of archetypal proportions. Like Phaethon, we appear to be oblivious to the extent of the devastation that our actions have created in the air, under the water, and upon the earth. Our actions include the facilities we operate, the materials we use and manufacture, and the lifestyles that support and validate this web of relations. Humanity has embarked upon its brief journey in a chariot of fire that we believe we can control. Proud of our divine connection, buoyed by the past successes of science, more than a little giddy about the opportunities for discovery, elated about the future, and virtually unconscious of the damage we daily deliver to the planet, we are – like Edward Teller – primarily concerned with how these laws of nature can be bent to serve the human will.

The picture that Barney paints is a dire one. With chart and graph, Barney is among many who can show how human activity damages the lands, seas, and skies. The greenhouse gases that we spew into the atmosphere have the effect of choking the entire community of creatures upon the planet. The truth is both inconvenient and uncomfortable for us – a bitter pill that inevitably humans must digest. The damage we do by plundering the seas is complicated by what we put into them: massive fishing depletes the supply of animal life, disrupting the balance of species, and shifting the ecology of our oceans and rivers. The toxins we dump into the deep combine with runoff from rivers and storm drain systems, destroying the sea's life-giving nature. As water temperatures rise, some species die while others migrate. The polar ice caps continue to melt – accelerating the rates of change, influencing the cycles of the seasons and the gravity of storm systems, and compelling plants, animals, and humans to adapt or become extinct. In many cases, entire species are being forced from the planet because they can adapt no further. As Gaia pleaded with Jove to deny Phaethon access to the Chariot of Fire, the earth is shouting loudly her cry of warning to a blind and self-serving human species.

According to Brian Swimme and Thomas Berry, the problem is our sense of identity, reflected in the discontinuity between the human and the nonhuman communities of the planet. Or as Pogo from the Walt Kelly comic strip of years ago said, "we have met the enemy and he is us."[61]

From culture to culture, faced with the opportunity for material gain or expansion, humans have created alliances, colonized and conquered one another – inventing ways to move goods and ideas around the planet. In the process, the Earth itself has become the resource base for human ingenuity and cultural sustenance. Confidence in our decision-making and unbridled optimism play out against the presumption of unlimited resources, which guides our chariot's course – blind to the devastating effects upon the Earth.

In *The Universe Story*, Swimme and Berry write:

The present disintegration of the life systems of the Earth is so extensive that we might very well be bringing an end to the Cenozoic period that has provided the identity for the life processes of Earth during the past sixty-seven million years ... the human has taken over such extensive control of the life systems of the Earth that the future will be dependent on human decision to an extent never dreamed of in previous times. We are deciding what species will live or perish. All this is filled with risk and presumption, pride, but if there is any way of guiding our course in such difficult decisions, it will be discovered only through an understanding of the most intimate aspects of the natural world.[62]

They suggest that we need to revisit our story and to see ourselves within the context of a much larger story, the story of the universe itself. This story has the potential to lead us out of our current course of destruction by reframing our relationship to nature by fostering a deep sense of communion. By seeing ourselves as a species within the family of all species, respect for the natural order may emerge. This respect holds the key to both our renewal and redemption. Swimme and Berry write that, "only a mythic vision can do this, since the universe itself can only be presented in a story with a mythic as well as a scientific aspect."[63]

The world of nature and the world of spirit may be brought into what Edward O. Wilson calls *consilience*, through a renewal of our imagination, our sense of wonder. This relation possesses both an inner and an outer aspect. The inner aspect is the context in which the outer aspect is grounded. The inner aspect requires a new mode of being in the world that is brought about by a transformation of consciousness. As that inner aspect develops, our sense of numinous wonder and appreciation of the natural world take on an entirely new and different character – where dialogue and interchange flow freely among the webs of inter-relation.

You have been invited to meet The Friend.
No one can resist a Divine Invitation.
That narrows down all our choices to just two:
We can come dressed for Dancing, or
Be carried on a stretcher to God's Ward.

Hafiz

PSYCHIC ENERGY
AND
THE STAGES OF TRANSFORMATION

Just after the devastation of the atomic bomb, the horror of the holocaust, and the unimaginable destruction of World War II, the Jungian Esther Harding wrote a treatise on the psychic energy of the primary instincts. She explores the critical need to understand those instincts as they relate to the evolutionary transformation of consciousness. In the preface to her book *Psychic Energy*, she writes:

> The surface, the façade of civilization, looks so smooth and fair; yet beneath the cultured mask of consciousness what savage impulses, what ruthless monsters of the deep await a chance to seize the mastery and despoil the world! [64]

Harding was inspired by our inhumanity and was motivated to bring greater awareness of the powers of the primary instinctual forces of life that she claims to be the instinct of self-preservation (security and survival), the instinct of self-reproduction (esteem and affection) and the instinct of self-gratification (power and control). These instinctual urges represent the gift of our evolutionary heritage that have been developed and refined over hundreds of millions of years.

The significant question that arises from reading *Phaethon* is whether humankind is capable of transforming itself beyond the basic, evolutionary aspects of these self-seeking urges. Can there be a transmutation of these instinctual urges into the noble ideals of civilized behavior? In a word, can we rise above greed, power, and control to develop our capacities for love, self-mastery, and mutual respect? Without a transformation of consciousness, "ruthless monsters of the deep" will continue to terrorize humanity and "despoil the world."

The alchemical myth of the mysterious transmutation of base metal into gold is based upon the use of fire as the healing element to instill change. Carefully applied, fire warms, cooks, and heals. Too much or too close, fire quickly scorches and turns beauty to ash. Alchemy suggests that as a place for transformation, the universe can be trusted as long as the processes of psychic functioning are carefully considered and humbly disciplined. In her study of human instincts and psychic energy, Harding suggests that we are caught somewhere in the middle of an unfolding story of consciousness, clearly face to face with the imminent need to develop a more acute spiritual perception.

Harding writes of three fundamental phases in the development of consciousness: the naïve stage of consciousness, the ego stage, and the consciousness of the Self.[65] She points out that in the evolutionary development of consciousness, each stage is subordinate to the next stage.

The first stage is largely unconscious and is totally dominated by the basic instincts: self-preservation, self-reproduction, and self-gratification. She designates this first stage "the autos," signifying a state of consciousness in which the person is compulsively directed by self-seeking instinctual urges, "completely dominated by auto-erotic desires."[66] Earlier, we wrote of this first stage as a state of *participation mystique*, an undifferentiated state of awareness, the total immersion of the ego in its natural animistic state.

The second stage emerged during the classical period, or Axial Age, when our reasoning faculties and powers of observation were being forged person by person. Harding remarks that,

> The ego becomes the center of consciousness, and the instinctive drives are modified through their relation to the new-found ego consciousness, which in its turn says 'I.' (Mankind's) attention is wholly directed to controlling his environment for his personal satisfaction and advantage. He has gained some control over his instinctive drives and for him the ego is now king; he classifies everything in terms of his own wishes, taking the good and rejecting the evil, not realizing that what he discards falls into the unconscious and does not cease to exist.[67]

Most of us live our lives from the centers of awareness of the first two stages, the autos and ego stages. The third stage of evolutionary development is the development of a conscious spiritual awareness. From earliest times until the present, this quest has proved elusive – challenging the rational capacities of humans to discover a core of divine substance around which they can weave their lives, find meaning, and sustain the enduring values of the world's great religious traditions. The exploration can take people into the mysteries of nature and the cosmos, as well as into the landscapes of the human imagination. This stage of development represents the goal or the work of spiritual transformation. Virtually every spiritual tradition suggests that meaning and happiness are possible only when the temptations of self-centered instinctual urges are mastered, when they are governed and directed by the altruistic urge of a higher Self.

Harding writes:

> In the third stage, the ego is displaced from its central position, becoming relative in importance to the new center of consciousness, the Self. Jung uses the term Self to represent the center of psychic awareness that transcends ego consciousness and includes in its scope all the vast reaches of the psyche that are ordinarily unconscious; it is therefore not only a personal consciousness but a nonpersonal one as well. Achievement of this level has been regarded by most of the great religions of the world as the supreme goal. It is expressed in such terms as 'finding the God within.'

> For the Self, the centre of this new kind of consciousness, is felt to be distinct from the ego and to possess an absolute authority within the psyche. It speaks with a voice of command exerting a power over the individual as

great as that of the instincts. When it functions strongly in a human being, it produces a preoccupation with the inner, subjective life that may appear to the onlooker to be auto-erotic self-absorption; but if the individual makes a clear differentiation between the personal self, the autos or the ego, and this center of nonpersonal compelling power, the activity is certainly not auto-erotic but reflects a concern with a superordinated value of the utmost significance for the development of the psyche and therefore also for mankind.[68]

The compelling power of the basic instincts in our lives is perhaps the driving issue of our historical moment. The forceful grip of these instincts upon each of us is often underestimated. Basic instincts play into the formulation of policy and decisions at the highest levels of business, social, and political culture – creating a climate for the marginalization of people and the justification to exploit nature in service to our own perceived personal and cultural needs. Harding writes:

We try to blind ourselves to the evidence of their (the primitive instincts) untamed power, and delude ourselves into believing that man's rational mind has conquered not only the world of nature around him but also the world of natural, instinctive life within.[69]

Harding's examination of primitive instincts fine-tuned over millions of years of evolutionary history makes it clear that these instincts have a self-referential nature, a life seemingly of their own that is concerned exclusively with the development of the species. In other words, it is as if human beings are the host for the instincts – the breeding ground for instinctual self-will. It bears paying attention to the "self" associated with each of these instincts: self-preservation, self-reproduction, and self-gratification. The element of self-interest associated with each of these instincts continues to be instrumental in perpetuating and proliferating the species known as *homo sapiens*, physically, mentally and socially. It is also clear that *homo sapiens* from the earliest stages of conscious awareness and creative expression has demonstrated itself to be self-centered and narcissistic in its perspective. Whether by design or convenience, since they first moved into the frames of their own conscious references, humans seem relentlessly drawn to gods in their own image – which by necessity subjugates the natural world over which the script humans create authorizes humans to have dominion.

This perspective has done much to promote a seemingly endless state of warfare among cultures as one group identifies those who oppose their expressed self-interests: East vs. West, North vs. South, Protestant vs. Catholic, Muslim vs. Jew, Sunni vs. Shia, and so on. We have yet to comprehend fully the scope of how dangerous the self-seeking nature of these instincts can be, especially now that throughout the world, nations, groups,  and individuals have the capability of manipulating nuclear energy, the solar force of Apollo. When the natural resources that one culture desires lie beneath the terrain of another, the environment becomes a victim – a pawn in the battle for access and control.

The scenario can lead to colonizing, occupation, conflict, and catastrophe. War and ruination of the earth to fulfill the instincts of self-perpetuation are indeed likely when the stage is set this way.

In his work with patients, C.G. Jung observed that humans possess other instincts in addition to the urges of self-preservation, self-reproduction, self-gratification, and the will to power. He differentiates "three other urges…the drive to activity, the reflection urge, and the so-called creative instinct."[70] As presented by Jung and his disciple Harding, the challenge is to transform the energy of the primitive urges into the art of living in community. They call for a high degree of social maturity by which egocentric desires rising from the bedrock of our instincts transform to serve the collective. They become the values and ideals of civilized community. Values such as compassion, justice, truth, love, and fairness embrace the other-than-human community as well.

As long as we are driven by unconscious, primal instincts, we are destined to perpetuate a legacy of violence, tragedy, and devastation upon the planet with increasing power. To the extent that we develop the skills to transmute those primal urges, there is hope for a better future and for a worldwide community of compassion. Harding writes:

> If any further step in the psychological development of man is to be taken, the exclusive domination of the conscious ego must be terminated, and the ruthless barbarism of the primitive instincts themselves must in some way be modified, so that their energy may be made available for the cultural advancement of the individual and in this way for society as well.[71]

Jung envisioned wholeness, individuation, and psychic integrity, as the goals of an evolved, meaningful human existence.

In his practice he encouraged his patients to pursue a path toward the wholeness that he believed was inherent and uniquely appropriate to every individual. He suggested that the roadmap to becoming conscious of our own wholeness and integrity existed as the fundamental characteristics of the psyche. In his own life he worked with the myth of alchemy as a way to see how the universe – including nature and the cosmos – supports and encourages this wholeness, not just for the human species but for the planet as well. Jung suggested that we adopt new modes of seeing that involve the capacities of imagination, integrating the panoply of the mind's psychic functions to reach the shores of spiritual value.

The Fall of Phaeton
Jan van Eyck (1395-1441)

A RESPONSE TO THE STORY

PHAETHON, SON OF APOLLO

Once we have read the story of Phaethon and reflected upon it, it is beneficial to allow for the heart's own response, one that engenders a sincere commitment to action. Phaethon stimulates an awareness of our cosmic connections because the human story has been so deeply influenced by its relationship with the Sun.

Can we see ourselves in the chariot? Can we feel the reins in our hands as we cling to the illusions of control over the powerful steeds? Can we feel Phaethon's fear as he recognizes his reach has far exceeded his grasp? Can we hear the cries of the earth and its inhabitants as our flight blazes its path of destruction across the planet? Can we awaken to our own inner voice of alarm and respond in time? Do we realize that – if we expect to pull out of our tailspin – nothing less than a complete transformation will do?

Ancient cultures were deeply mindful of the ego's potential to produce devastation it could not solve or heal. Their stories reflect their intuitive grasp of the basic aspects of human psychology and behavior. Phaethon's character, for example, stands as a warning against the excesses of pride. No amount of reasoning can explain or justify our current predicament – best described as our belief in our autonomy and in our immunity from the consequences of our actions, the subtle deception of specious liberty. Thus, caught between the will to solve any problems we might create and a nagging sense that we should change the course of human activity altogether, we are addressed by the story of Phaethon that prophetically reveals what lies ahead if the call is unheeded.

Phaethon's actions and ours mirror each another. We echo his attitude and seeming bravado. Our enthusiasm and haughty disregard for authority run parallel – both motivating the story and keeping it related to the human circumstance. Understandably, we feel a fascination with the story, for in the pool of wisdom of these ancient myths, the face we see reflected is our own. So what happens when we see a spark of recognition? Will the spark catch the fire of intention? Will we turn the course of human events in another direction, so as to become aware of both our own soul and the soul of the world, the *anima mundi*?

Narcissus
Caravaggio (1571-1610)
Galleria Nazionale d'Arte Antica
Rome, Italy

Poetry and art are windows to glimpse the essence of the Phaethon story. Poets and artists are often disguised prophets – creative souls who see the metaphorical qualities in nature and are gifted with the means to shape their creative expression to convey the subtle, often invisible, essences. For example, where the scientist measures time and space in quantifiable units, the poetic mind has the capacity to enter the fluid and unbounded nature of time and space – transforming the units of measurement into integers of inspiration, connection and complexity. Heraclitus realized the impermanence of time and space – that the birth and death of all things material are intimately interwoven. Thus, he said, "we never step into the same river twice." By coming to terms with the image of time and space as the faint echo of the universal, we may, as Blake suggests, "hold infinity in the palm of our hand, and eternity in an hour."[72]

In another poem, Hafiz, the 14th century Persian mystic, captures the spiritual depth of a beloved friend:

> One day the Sun admitted I am just a shadow
> I wish I could show you the Infinite Incandescence
> That has cast my brilliant image!
> I wish I could show you,
> When you are lonely or in darkness,
> The Astonishing Light
> Of your own Being![73]

Hafiz's poem speaks to invisible forces pre-existent to our sense of the external world. Contemporary philosophy, by and large, has continued to move further and further away from metaphysics, spiritual matters, or worldviews that allow nature its own voice. Whether focused narrow or broadly connective, somewhere along the way we either lost or gave up on the idea of "seeing the world in a grain of sand."[74] According to the great mathematician and philosopher, Bertrand Russell, such views are "non-sense." In other words, since there is no sensory verification of these realities, they are not worthy of serious philosophic discussion. Certainly, the aims and assumptions of ancient and contemporary philosophies differ.

Many thinkers through the ages and across cultures have felt compelled to acknowledge the immanence of governing invisible archetypal forces. Whether lying just behind the veil of what can be visibly seen or embedded in the expression of the physical world, thinkers the likes of Hafiz, Shankara, Lao Tzu, Socrates, Plato, Aristotle, Jesus, Mohammad, Thomas Aquinas, Maimonides, Al-Ghazzali, Kant, Goethe, Emerson, and William James have embraced the tireless task of moving through reality to glean both the divine substance and process within, above, beneath, and around. This view calls for a special quality of faith, a deep trust, for an experience of "seeing" beyond sensation. For a moment, let's look into the visible aspects of the long evolutionary story. Let's pull back the curtain of the timeline and peer behind the veil to see what has motivated our impressions. If we follow the image, the path may lead to response.

Out of the deep, my child, out of the deep,
From that true World within the world we see,
Whereof our world is but the bounding shore –

Alfred Lord Tennyson

THE VISIBLES

Give or take a few million years, about four and a half billion years ago, the sun gave birth to the Earth. Since that time, every morning the sun's rays emanate from the mother source of light and sustenance. The light takes approximately eight minutes to reach our planet. Without the sun, the Earth would be one of the countless, lifeless celestial bodies scattered through the heavens. Yet the sun brings vital warmth and initiates an incredible web of nourishment that connects all of the creatures in a complex pattern of interdependency. Every year, the Earth winds an elliptical path through deep space – spinning daily upon its axis and held in place by the sun's gravitational field. Our planet has been evolving for hundreds of millions of years. Species come and go, continents shift, and the waters rise and fall in a symphony of synergy and change. So far as we know, the Earth is unique. There is no other planet like the Earth anywhere in the universe.

Earth has been the character of continued alchemical transformation. Four and a half billion years ago, gaseous material erupted from the sun, carrying with it the potential for the formation of planets and life – on Earth or on any other planet with the right conditions. With the help of space travel, we now realize that Mars may have once had conditions suitable for the development of life, but it appears that Mars could not sustain those conditions. Similarly, it is not entirely clear whether Earth will always have the ability to sustain life. Recent scientific evidence suggests that human activity is taxing the earth's capacity for rejuvenation and protection.

One of the primary differences between Mars and Earth is that as far as we know, Mars has not been able to sustain the conditions for life, and no form of life has emerged to share or shoulder any part of the responsibility for sustaining life on Mars.

What separates Earth from Mars is that over time, an ecosystem has developed on Earth that includes humans. Although the evolutionary patterns of the Earth's myriad life forms have contributed to the growth and spreading of life around the planet, the sustainability of life today is threatened by human activity. Whether from mining, clearing of forests, drilling for oil, or filling the continents with civilizations, humans are disrupting the balances of nature and affecting the capacity of nature to respond. Accordingly, the future of the planet rests, in large part, on the heartfelt response and moral decisions of humans both individually and collectively. Billions of years of evolutionary development have led to the origin of *homo sapiens*; however, we are at risk of having the delicate balance of nature crumble like a house of cards within a few decades unless we motivate change in the way we as a species live on the earth.

In what can be considered a brief instant of evolutionary time, humans now seem to be actively engaged in the largest extinction of life in the history of Earth. Until now, there have been five great periods of extinction in the earth's long biological history: final Ordivician, late Devonian, final Permian (96% of all species perished), late Triasic, and final Cretaceous (the death of dinosaurs - 65 million years ago). As it is playing out, the scale of the current extinction will dramatically eclipse all the others!

For the vast majority of the time life has been present on Earth, life was expressed as minute, single-celled organisms living almost entirely in water and moisturized sediment. Only relatively recently, that is about 540 million years ago, did life begin to take on greater dimension, and only when just the right conditions coalesced. Billions of years preceded this emergence. About 350 million years ago, life began to move from its watery nursery onto the barren shores of the land, which even today occupies a small fraction of the Earth's surface. Ancient bacteria still work to support the conditions that make it possible for all larger forms of life to exist, including our own species.

In many ways, the consciousness that we have come to understand to be essential to our being human has the mixed blessing of separating us from the rest of creation – bestowing upon us a sense of personal autonomy and a psychological distance from the other life forms. To some extent, through rituals, metaphors, and symbols, we carve paths that enable some measure of return to the webs of our original interdependence. Yet fewer and fewer of us find the time or the inclination to seek ways to return to a deep involvement with nature. So for the most part today, our relations to nature and wild animals have become iconic – college mascots, corporate signage, and cultural toys having little to do with relating through deep bonds of animal

nature. Our dreams, art, and creative expression maintain the illusion of playful relationships with nature and animal worlds, but our naïveté grows as time and inexperience predominate. We have increasingly distanced ourselves from the matrix of our nature – both material and spiritual. Yet beneath the surface constructions of personality and cultural appearance, the archetypal character of life stirs in constant motion – a timeless continuation of patterns being expressed.

Do we feel our complementary and interdependent nature with all creation? Has our human experience become impoverished through our diminished capacity to communicate with the other-than-human world? Can we open ourselves to this larger perspective? As he was parsing the evolutionary patterns among life, Charles Darwin observed,

> There is grandeur in this view of life, with its several powers, having been originally breathed by the Creator into a few forms or into one; and that whilst this planet has gone cycling on according to the fixed law of gravity, from so simple a beginning endless forms most beautiful and most wonderful have been, and are being evolved.[75]

If we were to acknowledge the interdependent nature of all creation, would we take greater responsibility for the safeguarding of the rights and welfare of all beings on the planet, and not just those of the human species? If we were to realize the extent to which our actions threaten our survival, would we slow ourselves down or change course? Earth has a story that is continuing to unfold. Once that story is heard with depth and understanding, what will it take to motivate care and compassion for all nature and all species?

If all three realms are ruined – sea and land and sky –
Then we shall be confounded in old Chaos.
Save from the fire what's left, if anything can be saved.

Ovid

FOUR
ELEMENTAL
SPHERES

Over a period of hundreds of millions of years, fiery
meteors, asteroids, and planetesimals (rocky, often icy,
space bodies) crashed into the Earth's surface. Long before the
Earth had a protective atmosphere, these collisions etched the
signature of the solar system upon the Earth's surface and in doing
so brought matter and elements from the far reaches of the heavens.
In time the Earth's elements began to interact one with another
– resulting in what we call the *geosphere*. The geosphere grows
through steady accretion of matter and continues to be influenced
by the evolving character of its constitution. Like potter's clay,
the spherical shape and permeability of the Earth are a work in
constant process, molded by the power of the sun's gravity and the
energy of its transmission. During early historic time, enormous
volcanic activity made the Earth a fiery inferno – uninhabitable, a
cauldron in which the Earth's matter cooked and combined. We
find evidence of this time in the liquid states of matter just miles
beneath the planet's crust, still heated to thousands of degrees
Celsius, reflecting the epoch when the earth was intimately unified
with the sun. Yale geologist Richard Flint observes the continents

to be "a sort of granite raft floating in a sea of dark, heavy material, basaltic rock, which flows very slowly."[76] Beneath the basalt layer, we find the Earth's mantle and core – an even hotter *barysphere*: the center of the planet. Many believe the molecular constituents that gave rise to embryonic life poured forth from the uterine depths of the Earth, for as the earth began to cool, torrential storms were precipitated.

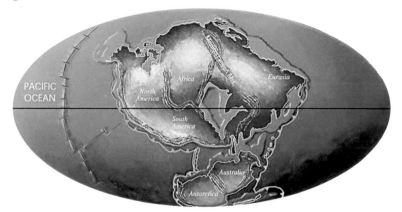

A magnificent ocean began to form from the accumulation of water that covered the earth billions of years ago – becoming the nursery of life known also as the *hydrosphere*. With the cooling and the release of gasses, a primitive *atmosphere* became increasingly capable of deflecting and withstanding the assaults of meteors and planetesimals. This created an insular, womb-like condition – ideal for the initiation and gestation of organic life.

Land originally did not conform to the continents we think of today, as you can see by the painting above. Fluid, shifting, and responsive to the earth's formative impulses, the tectonic plates moved across the surface like great hands seeking to arrange themselves around the pulse beating within. Emerging from beneath the ancient seas, these plates have always been in constant movement – beginning with the appearance of the early megacontinents, such as the Pangaea that sprawled across the equator before it divided into the continents as we see them today. These ancient land masses, or *lithosphere*, became the stage upon which life much later on would appear.

The Earth's early atmosphere consisted primarily of carbon dioxide, methane, ammonia, nitrogen, and water. From these complex molecules, organic constructions diverse and wonderful began to emerge – gathering and separating according to the natural principles of attraction and repulsion. The constant interaction of the Earth's inner core (the barysphere) with the sea (hydrosphere), land (lithosphere), and air (atmosphere) was nurtured by the heat and light of the sun. The convolution of these four elemental spheres has proven to be the alchemical gateway for the development of life on Earth: the *biosphere*. In alchemy, fire, air, earth, and water are known as the Four Sisters, continuing their communion with the sun to this day, promoting the conditions of life's vastness – within, above, below, and all around the planet.

The Psalmist proclaims this intimate communion:

> When I look up at the heavens, at the work of creation
> What is woman that you rejoice in her,
> And man that you do delight in him?
> You have made us in your image.
> You have made us co-creators of the earth!
> Guardians of the planet!
>
> To care for all your creatures,
> To tend the land, the sea, and the air we breathe;
> All that you have made,
> You have placed in our hands.
>
> --- *Psalm 8*

The heavens declare the glory of the Creator;
The firmament proclaims the handiwork of Love.

Psalm 19

THE PATTERNS OF LIFE

Read through the book of geological stone, the history
of planet Earth provides a breathtaking panorama of
the sweep of the evolution of life. Scientists are just beginning to
penetrate the real significance of the awesome patterns that emerge
from the wonder of Earth's geological text. When the translation of
the Earth's story evidenced in stone is confined to the boundaries
and literalism of pure science, the greater picture of an Earth
coming into its own character can easily be missed. Pure forensics
may capture the evidence of the Earth's early history, but the
patterns of evolution become evident only when viewed through
the softer lens of the questioning mind that asks "why" and "how"
in addition to "what." According to paleontologist Richard Fortey,
curator at the British Museum of Natural History, "life produces
patterns."[77] The evolution of the biosphere follows a pattern
similar to that of the geosphere: life emerges from fiery beginnings,
proliferates in the cool, salty waters of the ancient seas covering the
planet, crawls onto foreboding stretches of barren continents that
emerged above those seas, and thrives and grows in the oxygenated
atmosphere of a time out of memory. Both the geosphere and
the biosphere reflect inward and external conditions, and they are
deeply implicated in each another's development and maturation.
In a word, they inter-penetrate.

Recovering the wonder and reverence for the Earth's

primordial beginnings is essential to sustaining life on this fragile planet, particularly if the intent of humanity is neither to deny the extent of the Earth's fragility nor to leave the future of the Earth to chance. Only when we situate the human species within the scope of evolutionary history can we become responsible and compassionate stewards of the environment. Once our perspective transcends the limits of self-admiration, self-assertion, and opportunism, we can begin the process of nurturing humanity's greatest gifts: our capacity for self-reflection and an evolved moral sense that extends past the priorities of the human species to care for all existence on the planet. For unless we establish the Earth as a priority, the rest will be moot.

Paleontologist Stephen Jay Gould reminds us that with respect to evolution, we must first accept once and for all that "we are of it, not above it."[78] We are embedded in the story of the planet and the universe and as such, we need to learn, embrace, and share this story because it is the centerpiece of our narrative as a species.

Both the healing elixir and transforming balm of cosmic consciousness are contained within an understanding of the evolutionary story. In his book *Life on a Young Planet*, Harvard paleontologist Andrew Knoll writes:

> Science's creation story is a deeply engrossing narrative that, told correctly, helps us to understand not only our biological past, but the Earth and life that surround us today. Contemporary biological diversity is the product of nearly 4 billion years of evolution. We are a part of this legacy. Thus, by coming to grips with life's long evolutionary history, we begin to understand something of our own place in the world, including our responsibility as planetary stewards.[79]

When you were an Amoeba
And I was a Paramecium
So many eons ago
In the briny deep we swam
Enjoying the Precambrian flow.

Our cares were few
As volcanoes raged
Above the salty brew
Geologic forces, totally engaged.

When you were an Ammonite
And I was a Trilobite
Five hundred million years ago
In the briny deep we flourished
Upon Cambrian mud we nourished.

Our cares were few
As earthquakes raged
And continents grew and grew
Providing me and you, a whole new stage!

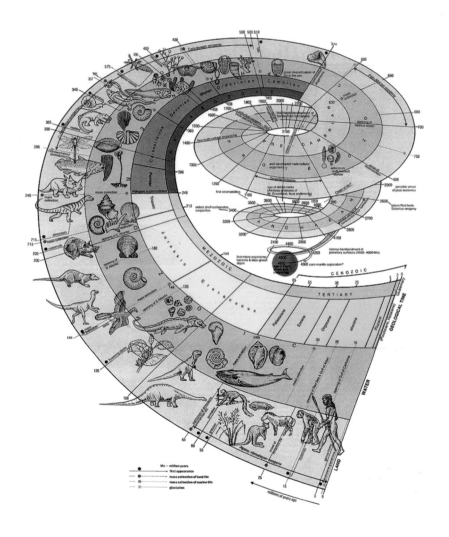

The centipede was happy, quite,
Until the toad for fun
Said, "pray, which leg comes after which?"
This worked his mind to such a pitch
He lay distracted in a ditch, considering how to run.

Anonymous

EVOLUTIONARY PATTERNS
AND
A FRAME OF REFERENCE

In his 1915 textbook, *Historical Geology*, Yale professor of paleontology Charles Schuchert wrote:

> Life, once started out of water and carbon dioxide, has
> gone on ceaselessly, striving through force of circumstances
> toward better adapted mechanisms endowed with higher
> and higher thinking powers.[80]

Schuchert suggests that life not only represents an evolution of biological mechanisms adapted for physical survival, but more importantly also reflects the evolution of consciousness itself. Consciousness appears to be the heart of the evolutionary process, directly correlating with the ability of a species to survive, influencing reactions, enabling memory and meaning, and arguably the prime mover of evolution.

From the early emergence of the notochord – the tube within a tube – to the articulation of a backbone and the development of the brain, evolution viewed from a human perspective seems to be as much about the development of the capacity for awareness and intelligence as about anything else. In order to appreciate the full extent of this implication, scientists had best become poets, while poets would do well to develop a systematic appreciation of the complexities observed in the scientific disciplines.

Pierre Teilhard de Chardin, the twentieth-century Catholic theologian, paleontologist, and philosopher who had as much invested in refuting Darwin's evolutionary theories as anyone else, came to regard the world as a dynamic expression of evolutionary development characterized by dialectical thresholds and ordered stages. In *The Phenomenon of Man*, Teilhard identifies three primary stages:

1) the geosphere, the development of inorganic aspects of the Earth, a growth that is sustained through the outward process of accretion, and the dynamic interaction of Earth's barysphere, hydrosphere, lithosphere and atmosphere;

2) the biosphere, the development of the organic aspects of the planet, a growth that is sustained by an inward self-organizing process, autopoesis. The biosphere represents an envelope of life surrounding the planet;

3) and, the noosphere, the development of consciousness, a process that is supported by a dynamic interaction of

both inward and outward processes. The noosphere represents an envelope of consciousness surrounding the planet.[81]

Seeing the Earth's evolution as movement from geosphere to consciousness is compatible with traditional views such as Schuchert and Teilhard, as well as with more advanced biological and paleontological perspectives, such as Richard Fortey, who writes in his book *Life*:

> The history of life can be thought of as a crossing of thresholds – each threshold allowing more freedom for further biological growth and change. The first, replicating molecules producing living cells – these cells then collaborating in tissues and organisms – and, later, sexual differentiation promoting enhanced rates of change; the colonization first of the land, and then of the air, which life itself had manufactured.

> But then the final threshold is consciousness, freeing the mind from the confines of mere cells, allowing imagination to probe situations not yet encountered: a sense of self – and reason – are those properties we like to consider uniquely human. Was this a species character, like the plumage of a pheasant or bird of paradise, or the spots on a leopard? It is the uniqueness of this threshold which allows this one species a disproportionate place in my narrative: Man the Thinker, the sapient one.[82]

In *The Phenomenon of Man* Teilhard suggests that, more than an additional theme, consciousness is the central purpose in the development of evolution, the source of the autopoetic dynamic. Evolution is the language of consciousness – the way the *anima mundi* communicates itself. Seen thus, humans become one of the many hosts whose mission in life is to serve the greater good of the *anima mundi*. Teilhard regards the advent of self-reflection, Apollonian consciousness, within *homo sapiens* as an epochal threshold in evolution. He writes:

> The being who is the object of his own reflection becomes in a flash able to raise himself into a new sphere. In reality, another world is born. Abstraction, logic, reasoned choice and inventions, mathematics, art, calculation of space and time, anxieties and the dream of love – all these activities of inner life are nothing else than the effervescence of the newly-formed center as it explodes onto itself.[83]

Certainly, the immediate flash of self-awareness is startling to the individual – whether the awareness takes place in the childhood of a person or in that of a species. If the first inclination is to turn back into the womb of *participation mystique*, where the individual and the collective are inseparable, the awareness of the self does not disappear even with attempts to quash or deny its existence. That newly formed center is the birth of the ego, the seed from which evolution migrates toward civilization, toward institutions whose mission is to pursue scientific, philosophic and religious truths, toward affiliations committed to creative expression, and toward the democracy of ideas the purpose of which is reverence for life through service and communion. Civilization is ideally the expression of that prime impulse to reflect upon circumstances and to move forward with compassion, courage, and a concern for the well being of the civilization's denizens.

Time, like that stream, moved on
As brains overtook the brawn
Our reptilian brain subsiding
Furry young mammals became we.

For all of our sighs
How our joys did rise
With the sight of our little ones
Playing with sticks and stones.

When you were a Pithecus
And I was a little cuss,
How exciting when our tribe did gather
Looking out from our caves above
Sharing the faint glimmer of that thing called love!

Four Sisters - Alchemy
Adam MacLean

Your enjoyment of the world is never right
'Til every morning you awake in heaven,
See yourself in your Father's palace,
And look upon the skies, the earth, and the air
As celestial joys!

Thomas Traherne

THE FOUR SISTERS AT HOME

Life on Earth is woven from four unique elements: earth itself, along with air, fire, and water – mixed in intimate proportion, relation, and communion with the heat and light of the sun. Consider the four inorganic spheres: the the lithosphere, the atmosphere, barysphere, and the hydrosphere. We observe each and all interacting to bring forth the pleroma of the biosphere that in turn creates its own profound effects upon the geosphere, setting the stage for further evolution of the planet and ultimately incubating and fostering consciousness. "Life and environment comprise one linked system; they have an umbilical connection."[84]

For the first natural philosophers, the four elements of earth, air, fire, and water were the language of their world – the voice that articulated the human condition as they listened the only way they knew. The recognition and appreciation of the four elements helped to express the experience of heat and cold, dryness and moisture. Individualized ego-centered consciousness began to forge a separation of self from the natural world. The delineation of the four natural elements was a monumental first step in interpreting the world through its natural relations, and in seeing the continuity, character, and stability of change. In the West, the project of developing individualized consciousness may have begun in ancient Greece when the pre-Socratic philosophers first observed natural substances to exist in opposition to one another, when Pythagoras framed the elegance of what he called a mathematically ordered "cosmos." The philosopher Empedocles furthered our understanding of the natural world, regarding earth, air, fire and water as four irreducible elements – the organizing

 principles around which all existence is composed, moving apart by "strife" or creating attraction by "love," giving rise to everything.

Today in scientific as well as philosophical circles, we have come to a renewed appreciation and respect for how the ancients discovered and expressed the interrelations of these four elements. We now see that they are the architectural building blocks of every environment we inhabit and profoundly influence our lives in ways that we are just now realizing. We are becoming aware of the work of each organic cell as it transforms and delivers the fiery energy received from the sun. We are conscious that the fluid pouring through our veins was once the ocean that was home and nursery. We are now mindful that we are literally "of the soil and the soil of us," as the Sioux Indians would say. And, with every breath we take, we recognize that the atmosphere lives within us and we live within the atmosphere, that life subsists on air as it does on the fire of the sun, wellsprings of fresh water, and the nutrients of earthy fecundity.

The mystery and heart of life's story are that life presents images of what can be called autopoetic nests that express the dynamic principles of unity and diversity. According to philosopher

Ken Wilber, evolution organizes autopoetically, building upon itself in the image of

> a series of nests within nests within nests. Each higher
> level of complexity possesses the essential features of its
> lower levels, but then adds elements not found on those
> levels. Each higher level... transcends but includes its
> juniors. And this means that each level of reality has a
> different architecture.[85]

The nest is but another name for *home* – a metaphorical way to suggest that evolution is a way to develop home, to feel at home on a fragile, often dangerous planet. Wilber's view suggests hierarchical levels of complexity in the story of life, where stages build upon and incorporate preceding stages. Even with occasional twists in the road, this evolution produces a home that is responsive to the current conditions of the Earth's environment, that while it shapes, it is constantly being shaped by, that environment. Andrew Knoll points out that "even a casual observer will notice the pattern of nested similarity displayed by Earth's biological diversity."[86]

Thomas Berry is a historian of world cultures and religions, an environmental activist, and a self-described "geologian." He writes about life on Earth as "an irreversible sequence of transformation moving from a lesser to a greater order of complexity and from a lesser to greater consciousness."[87] Worldviews that incorporate similar ideas of nests can be found in Chinese and Indian thought as well as in the Hermetic traditions, such as alchemy, of the West.

With the advent of the Scientific Revolution, "the enlightenment," ridding the world of its mystery has been both the goal and consequence of the progression of consciousness. Qualitative sensibilities gave way to quantitative valuations of time and space – leading to a valuation of abundance, accumulation, and ownership. Soul became replaced by a fascination with force, speed, energy, and power. On the one hand, the analysis of reality into its constituent components advances the facility of human consciousness – enabling the human mind to form categories, make associations, and discover meaning. On the other hand, each new discovery and every new theory awaken new possibilities and open new doors to unanswered questions and unsolved connections. Mystery, it seems, is nested into the very fabric of evolution and will not disappear – except perhaps through indifference.

Mystery fuels human self-understanding and provides untold collateral benefit as a sacred well of nourishment and transformation. It seems that for all our material progress, we are compelled to return to an experience of the cosmos that is both our origin and our destination. In *Four Quartets*, T.S. Eliot says it best:

We shall not cease from exploration
And the end of all our exploring
Will be to arrive where we started
And know the place for the first time.
Through the unknown, remembered gate
When the last of earth left to discover
Is that which was the beginning;
At the source of the longest river
The voice of the hidden waterfall
And the children in the apple-tree
Not known, because not looked for
But heard, half-heard, in the stillness
Between two waves of the sea.
Quick now, here, now, always –
A condition of complete simplicity
(Costing not less than everything)
And all shall be well and
All manner of thing shall be well.[88]

Love is my light and my salvation, whom shall I fear?
Love is the strength of my life, of whom shall I be afraid?

Psalm 27

THE COSMOGENETIC PRINCIPLE –
THREE THEMES

Cosmogenesis expresses the viewpoint that the universe is both a cosmos guided by a universal principle of order and an eternal genesis that is creatively exhibiting both mystery and a compelling quality of adventure.

The Cosmogenetic Principle is expressed by three themes of life's primary evolutionary process: *autopoesis, differentiation,* and *communion.* What do they mean? The three fundamental principles form the basis of a new myth that is a way to understand who we are. *Autopoesis* provides identity and presence. *Differentiation* expresses diversity and distinction. *Communion* reveals kinship and interdependence. Each idea represents an approach – cosmic words, *logoi,* that apply to all of us and make sense as a system for navigating purposefully. Properly understood, they call for a response. Why? Because together, these three principles are the cornerstones of cosmogenesis, without which authentic existence is not possible.

As Brian Swimme points out, "cells brought *autopoesis* (the power of self-organization), *differentiation* (the power of creative diversity), and *communion* (the unity inherent in existence) to new levels which made up for their fragility and enabled them to endure."[89] The three themes set the character and tone for conscious existence and are therefore integral to situating oneself and moving mindfully and purposefully.

Swimme elaborates:

These three terms—differentiation, autopoesis, and communion—refer to the governing themes and the basal intentionality of all existence. Some synonyms for differentiation are diversity, complexity, variation.

Different words that point to the second feature (autopoesis) are subjectivity, self-manifestation, sentience, self-organization, dynamic centers of experience, presence, identity, inner principle of being, voice, interiority.

And for the third feature, communion, interrelatedness, interdependence, kinship, mutuality, internal relatedness, reciprocity, complementarity, interconnectivity, and affiliation.[90]

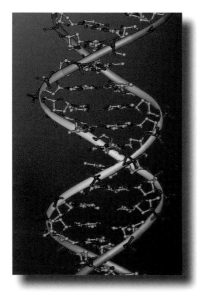

Biochemists consider adenine, thymine, guanine, and cytosine to be the genetic building blocks, the code or chemical programming of life. It is DNA that gives expression through its alphabet to the language of the cosmogenetic principle. DNA is essential to the establishment and evolution of all life and offers a window into an organism's uniqueness, purpose, and affiliation with all other organisms. Any variation in the DNA affects the cellular construction and content which in turn affects the organism. Differentiation, autopocsis, and communion form the language that helps to unlock the questions: where do we come from, why are we here, and where are we going? Without these archetypal drives, the evolution of consciousness would simply not take place and the process would dissolve and dissipate. These principles express our diversity, the value of interiority, and the magnificent inter-connection we each have to the story of life's unfolding. It is no coincidence that variation, identity, and complementarity are among the dominant themes of cultural expressions – playing themselves out in cultural values, art, politics, and religion. Today, their impact upon the environment is being felt as increased emphasis is placed upon the symbols and cultural manifestations that address a person's variation, identity, and complementarity. There is little question that life today represents an expanding panorama of differentiation. What is more, where in times past a person might be aware of surrounding communities, today awareness of the inter-relatedness of Earth's peoples and places is commonplace, if not ubiquitous. The rural tribesperson might know more about the art and culture of the urban landscape than the local suburbanite does. Life continues to broaden its scope and reach through behaviors that are activated within the organism and propagated by a network of support systems. Very often, these conditions are the justification for putting natural resources into service for the benefit, convenience, and profit of people. All across the planet, cultures interact and participate in a global exchange of goods, ideas, and influences. As a species, we have become increasingly aware of our interdependence and intimate links with all the other forms of life. Our future and well-being are implicated in the future and well-being of the planet.

As a result of the autopoetic impulse of life it is estimated that we, as one species, dwell on a planet that has experienced a differentiation of millions of species of life. Our scientists "have classified on the order of two million species of life. Biologists estimate there may be ten to thirty million species altogether"[91] The two million species that we are aware of include "some eight hundred and fifty thousand species of insects . . . five hundred thousand species of round worms," three hundred and fifty thousand species of plants, and forty thousand vertebrate species of which there are "four thousand five hundred mammalian species."[92] In some mysterious manner, each of these species is related to every other species – they all share a common ancestor.

The Cosmogenetic Principle may be summed up in one of the most important insights of the alchemical tradition, known as the Hermetic Formula:

> Nature is delighted by another Nature (communion, interrelatedness, affiliation); and Nature is contained by another Nature (subjectivity, interiority, autopoesis); and Nature knows how to surmount Nature (differentiation, diversity, complexity).[93]

The Hermetic Formula suggests that there is a certain play in the interrelations of nature in which we observe the interdependence of all life; the mysterious depth of nature appears to express itself autopoetically; nature evolves through a dynamic differentiation and artistic complexity, a crossing of thresholds, all of which appears to manifest what Swimme calls "basal intentionality."[94] These three cosmogenetic themes articulate the invisibles underwriting the visibles – the great mystery of what Einstein refers to as "the Illimitable Superior Spirit."

One of the significant developments of evolutionary time that began approximately 2.5 billion years ago that demonstrates the Cosmogenetic Principle at work was the emergence of a miraculous new way for nature to capture the sun's energy – photosynthesis. Imagine being able to catch a fastball of light from the sun, moving at 186,000 miles per second! Swimme describes this spectacular moment:

> Another mutation (differentiation) appeared that is one of the greatest acts of creativity in the four billion years of the living Earth. This mutation took the porphyrin ring ... twisted it in conjunction with other chemicals (autopoesis) and

discovered a molecular net with the power to capture photons in flight. This mutation had the ability to convert the energy of a particle rifling through the air at the speed of light into the molecular structures of food. Suddenly a new intimacy (communion) was established between Earth's living surface and the radiant energy from its central star.[95]

The capacity of converting the light of the sun into life energy would fuel virtually every move in evolution since – demonstrating "the wild wisdom at the heart of the universe story."[96] Fortey writes of the monumental significance of photosynthesis: "What drives the whole ecological engine is energy – energy derived from the sun and fixed in photosynthesis. Everything else depends upon it."[97] As Blake suggests, we begin to see a wondrous sense of basal intentionality behind a grain of sand, in the wild flower, and in touch of a newborn child:

> To see a World in a grain of sand,
> And Heaven in a wild flower,
> Hold infinity in the palm of your hand
> And Eternity in an hour...
> Joy and woe are woven fine,
> A clothing for the soul divine;
> Under every grief and pine
> Runs a joy with silken twine...
>
> He who doubts from what he sees
> Will ne'er believe, do what you please.
> If the Sun and Moon should doubt,
> They'd immediately go out...
>
> God appears, and God is Light...[98]

Through an enchanted gateway of autopoetic splendor, humanity is invited to experience the depth of its own interiority, seemingly infinite and eternal in dimension. This invitation allows us to touch and be transformed by the presence that some call "God," others "the Self," and still others "the One." Out of that inner experience of our own being emerges a creative and ethical response, a commitment to the multitude of relationships that one discovers in that secret garden – relationships that extend to every corner of the planet, to both human and other-than-human communities. As we connect with the sun of our own being, we become infused with qualities of wisdom and compassion that allow for creative expression, co-partnership with an ongoing genesis story. Within the experience of the underlying unity of our diversity lies the promise of personal and collective evolution.

Be warned and understand truly
That two fishes are swimming in our sea,
The vastness of which no man can describe.
Moreover the Sages say that the two fishes are one;
They are two, and nevertheless they are one.

The Book of Lambspring

EVOLUTIONARY INSTINCTS

Jungian psychologist Edward Edinger explored human
evolution – considering both the psychological and the
scientific aspects – as an operation of increased consciousness
arising from a creative resolution of two oppositional forces within
the consciousness of our species. In other words, humans are a
species that learns from experience – building skills, memory, and
the capacity for reasoning that are the essential building blocks
of consciousness. Both Jung and his disciple Edinger put their
professional focus on the human species, but each in his own way
addressed the spectra of archetypal expressions that are indigenous
to all species of life. Chinese wisdom speaks of the creative forces of
yin and yang. Indian wisdom speaks of tamas and rajas, oppositional
energies. The Greek philosopher Empedocles referred to the forces
of love and strife.

Edinger writes that, "the opposites constitute the most
basic anatomy of the psyche. The flow of libido, or psychic
energy, is generated by the polarization of opposites in the same
way as electricity flows between the positive and negative poles
of an electrical current."[99] Currents of oppositional energy run
dynamically down the canal of evolutionary time, giving birth to a
wondrous plethora of living forms. Autopoetic energy authors the

expression of life as a biological process through which every living thing becomes what it is destined to become. Aristotle referred to the subjective movement of organic growth as *entelechy*, the drive for all life forms to blossom into their own unique selves. Jung took the process a step further, describing individuation as that organizing principle that brings wholeness to a particular soul. We individuate our own archetypal patronage – which may explain why following another's drumbeat courts disaster and the potential of failing to fulfill one's own true nature.

We began to ask why
With a story and a sigh
We'd share our travails of the day
Howling across the moonlit bay!

Alchemy is based upon concepts or processes called *coniunctio* - bringing opposing elements into conjunction to create something novel while retaining the individuality of the constituent components. While there continues to be a great deal of misunderstanding about alchemy, scholars now realize that even for the chemists of the Middle Ages, alchemy involved much more than laboratory concoctions, mixtures, and formulas. A central insight of alchemy was that the "person" implementing the procedures and the context in which the procedures are occurring must be factored into the outcome. The "person" was precisely the element that science sought to overcome or eliminate as it embarked upon the quest for objectivity – statements and conditions that were neither influenced nor tainted by personal involvement or context. More and more, scientists are coming to realize that even the most judicious experiments are contextualized – and rather than seeking to account for or overcome subjectivity, they are learning to incorporate it.

Alchemy can be understood as an expression of the manner in which the opposing energies of the psyche evolve dialectically within the structures of life in increasingly growing autopoetic complexity and splendor. The self differentiates its own internal relatedness. As Esther Harding writes, "with the development of the psyche through the centuries, control over the instincts gradually increased. Bit by bit they were changed, losing to a certain extent their automatic and compulsory character, so that the individual gained increasing freedom of choice and of action."[100] For an amoeba, there is extreme compulsion in its character and behavior as it engages a never-ending drive to preserve its existence.

With the relatively recent advent of sexuality in cellular organisms, new instincts and compulsions not surprisingly emerge.

However, in chimps and other marsupials we observe increasing freedom from compulsion – a reflection of choice, one of the seeds  of early consciousness and crucial to the development of empathy. And so it is for humans. Harding suggests that we can trace our own instincts up through the evolutionary line to the mammalian species of *Homo sapiens*. She observes that "these instinctual powers are more ancient than the psyche of man, being rooted in the very substance and nature of the living organism, in the essence, the spirit, the life of protoplasm itself. For this reason they dominate the functioning of all living creatures."[101]

Tensions between the compulsive nature of our instincts and our imagined sense of freedom have created many of the difficulties we face today. In the past, the contexts of humanity were more or less able to absorb abuses to the environment and cultures at war. For the most part, the human footprint could not affect the earth to the extent that nature could not rebound, adapt, and continue on. However, with population outstripping the earth's capacity to sustain human involvement, with damage to nature surpassing crisis proportions, we are called to respond and alter our ways. Hope for the future lies in the creative resolution of these tensions. Harding's inspiration for addressing these tensions emanated from her observation of two catastrophic world wars in which millions tragically died, most of whom were civilians. Primitive instincts continue to dominate much of our political will and private ambition, setting the stage for new tragedies.

Harding writes:

Life first appeared on earth, so far as we know, in the form of single living cells. From these simple origins all other life forms developed. Today, the Earth is covered with living organisms, constituting the whole of the vegetable and animal kingdoms.

They are all descendants of those small, pregnant original cells that lived and died millions of years ago. The same physical and chemical laws that controlled the life processes of those ancestral forms still govern the physiology of the complex animals of the present day. In the psychological sphere too, far removed as this is from those simple beginnings, many reminders of the ancient life patterns survive to affect the attitudes and habits of modern man, although he usually remains quite unaware of their influence.[102]

When you were the Princess
And I was the Prince
In great castles, not so long ago
We pined for adventure
Sailing upon the Mediterranean flow.

Our hearts did quest
As battles we fought
To become the kingdom's best
Then, 'twas our glory we sought!'

Agreeing with Harding in her assessment of the human condition as deeply influenced by the primordial instincts of the unconscious, Jung writes that "since time immemorial man has needed the transformation mysteries to turn him into something, to rescue him from the animal collective psyche."[103] His endorsement of the alchemist's appreciation of nature stemmed from his observation that psychic transformation is concealed in nature and that, as such, nature is the home of metamorphosis, the jewel in the crown of consciousness, and represents the hope of redemption and salvation for humanity.

Jung introduced a new term that he employed to express the deepest layers of consciousness: *the psychoid*. The psychoid dwells at the heart of the autopoetic impulse, existing in relations between consciousness and the unconscious, a kind of threshold or liminal zone, the shoreline of the soul where the deep waters of the unconscious do their work.

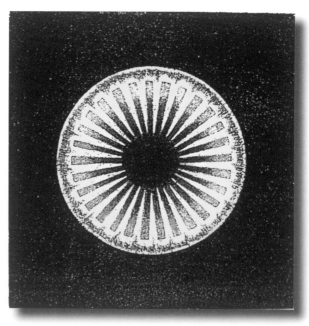

He writes:

Just as a man has a body which is no different in principle from that of an animal, so also his psychology has a whole series of lower storeys in which the specters from humanity's past epochs still dwell, then the animal souls from the age of pithencanthropus and the hominids, then the 'psyche' of the cold-blooded saurians, and, deepest down of all, the transcendental mystery and paradox of the sympathetic and parasympathetic psychoid systems.[104]

Here, in the psychoid, the archetypes that are the source and propensity of human nature make their home, providing the driving force of nature's evolutionary panorama. These autopoetic forces contribute to understanding and enhance our ability to survive in nature as denizens of the earth. Others emerge as dreams and imaginative inclinations toward the supernatural and divinity – the quest for heaven. The story of the growth of consciousness on Earth is one that closely mirrors the story of evolution. Evolution certainly does not begin with the human species, and, it will not end with humanity regardless how we respond to our current condition. My own mentor, paleontologist Dr. Raymond M. Alf, captures the moment of self-consciousness with poetic prescience:

Protohuman knelt for an imbibition of moisture to slacken a thirst. Behold – a reflection in the still water, an image, a face whose piercing eyes penetrated to something deep inside. There was born a subliminal idea of a spirit dwelling within. Our being spoke to the face in the mirror. There was no answer. The lips moved as if to reply, and there was a strange response. It was a still small voice within whispering: 'Build thee more stately mansions.'

A plethora of images flashed through the mind. There was a picture of primordial ooze at the dawn of creation, back, back some time three billion years plus. The distillation of dissimilar constituents brought forth change, a continuous struggle to surpass the biological present and innovate a never-ending state of becoming.

There came a sense perception of a time long gone. Dim visual representations of the past gave way gradually to a *tableau vivant*. Out of the water; on to the land; up into the trees and down again; standing upright; grasping tools; group protection; family bonding; learning; insight; foresight; and now, personal awareness—Who am I?[105]

Dare we examine these moments and ask about the development of our human instincts? Dare we interrogate the role that these instincts may have in our responsibility to tend and serve the environment? Consciousness and self-consciousness emerged in a concomitant fashion – joined at the heart of the context. With our self-consciousness, we have become endowed with the capacity to confront the serious questions regarding our responsibility for nature and one another. The myths and stories of ancient cultures are imbued with an intuitive grasp that these questions underwrite life's meaning and purpose. C.G. Jung, Esther Harding, Raymond Alf, Marie-Louise von Franz, and numerous others implore that we not only ask the hard questions but also respond. Jung writes about the evolution of the psyche:

> Every civilized human being, however high his conscious development, is still an archaic man at the deeper levels of his psyche. Just as the human body connects us with the mammals and displays numerous vestiges of earlier evolutionary states going back even to the reptilian age, so the human psyche is a product of evolution which, when followed back to its origins, shows countless archaic traits.[106]

From single-celled organisms, all other life forms evolved.
As different as humans, plants, and animals are, every cell of
every organism, small and large, on the planet carries the same
basic biologic structure. The laws of physics and chemistry that
controlled the life processes of those early days of single-celled
creatures still regulate the more complex forms of life that roam the
planet today. Along with the evolution of physical and biological
structures, there has arisen in humans a corresponding complexity
of psychic structure with its corresponding laws. For billions of
years, that psychic structure was dominated by the basic urges of
security and survival, esteem and affection, power and control.
Only within the last few thousands of years did the human species
in particular become conscious of the motivating power of those
instinctual urges.

Reflection is the process of self-consciousness at work
– and whether we observe reflection in the myth of Narcissus or
elsewhere, the capacity for reflection marks a new chapter in the
evolutionary story of the psyche. It is a monumental milestone
when, for the first time, a species is capable of carving out its
character so as to shape its destiny in the story of evolution.
Through honest and conscious reflection, one may observe how
primordial instincts are manifest in the institutions of culture
and in the behaviors of individuals regardless of culture and
background. The narrative of the human species moving toward the
development of civilization evokes the growth of social institutions
arising from our primordial instinctual urges, institutions that
while addressing those urges to a greater or lesser degree have
now become forces unto themselves that are calling for humans to
exercise judgment, governance, and restraint.

Now here we sit
Sharing stories of wit
Remembering our lives long ago,
Dreaming mythically of our future
Of our soul's precious nurture.

Our cares have grown and grown
As nations now rage
From every corner of earth a moan
Political forces, totally engaged!

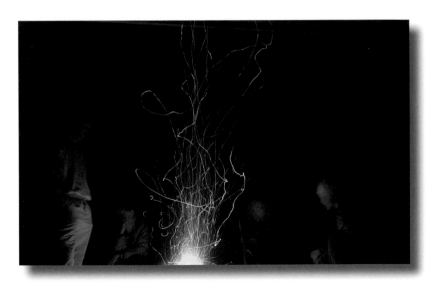

The instincts for security and survival are fundamental to the creation and sustenance of communal and commercial institutions of all cultures. Increasingly, the evolution of the survival instinct has been confronted by an awareness of the interdependent nature of all existence. The instincts of esteem and affection are evidenced in the social institutions of culture; the concept of family is affected by geography, economics, and the traditions of particular cultures. The instincts of power and control manifest themselves as a movement toward government and regulatory institutions. The impulses for order and organization in personal and collective circumstances range from monarchy to democracy, and can be characterized by deep fear and alienation as well as a developed sense of trust and connection. Today, as economic forces drive government and regulatory decisions, the private sectors of business play an increasingly political role, displaying how our instinctual drives intersect in their movement toward wholeness. Cultural evolution is a story of often competing but generally cooperative behaviors that over time effectively utilize social institutions to identify, create, and sustain a society's needs and desires.

Much of the last four to five centuries of thought can be seen as a conscious reflection upon the human condition. As the medieval period transformed through the Renaissance to the modern period, the pendulum of philosophic thought swung from theology to science and from things spiritual to material. Philosophy was no longer the handmaiden of religion; it became the wench of science – as much a plaything as a mistress to dress up when science needed legitimacy to broker its projects for the public eye. As the role of philosophy and religious thought were transformed, Enlightenment thinkers such as René Descartes and John Locke were profoundly affected by the individual's capacity to associate ideas, to think for himself, and to separate himself from nature and others. Thus, the mottos of the time became "I think, therefore I am" and "think for yourself."

During the nineteenth century, philosophers began to examine the political aspects of the human condition more closely in order to uncover the inwardly rooted causes of our instinctual urges. From a perspective that has become known as dialectical materialism, Karl Marx sought to frame the idea of social justice for community by articulating the prime motives for our economic and political agenda, which he took to be our need for security and survival. Friedrich Nietzsche believed that the drive of our will to self-actualize as we gravitate upwards to greater power and control was central to the human condition. In *Thus Spake Zarathustra*, he asks: "what urges you on and arouses your ardour? You put your will and your values upon the river of becoming; what the people believe to be good and evil betrays to an ancient will to power."[107] Sigmund Freud put the accent upon our instinctual needs for esteem and affection, our sexual identity. Richard Tarnas writes about the significance of Freud's impact: "Man could no longer doubt that it was not only his body but his psyche as well for which powerful biological instincts – amoral, aggressive, erotic – were the most significant motivating factors."[108]

However powerful each of these perspectives is on its own, each is as partial as it is myopic. As Jung observes, the human condition presents a tension between two polarities: spirit and matter, heaven and earth. Neither can be rejected, and both must be engaged in order that the creative tension be maintained and for an alchemical transformation of the psyche to go forth. The great challenge is to see the ancient, primordial instincts of our evolutionary heritage in relation to what Jung calls the archetypal light of the human condition. As far as humanity has progressed, we inevitably find ourselves returning to our beginnings.

> God has indeed made an inconceivably sublime and
> mysteriously contradictory image of himself, without the help
> of man, and implanted it in man's unconscious as an archetype,
> the archetypal light in order that the unpresumptuous man
> might glimpse an image, in the stillness of his soul.[109]

When you are a Cherubim
And I am a Seraphim
So many eons from now
Across galactic time we'll roam
Calling the entire cosmos our home.

Our anxieties will be few
As we move in spirit anew
Our stories to share of a day long ago
When you were an Ammonite and I was a Trilobite!

High mountains, deep waters, and a dense jungle of grass –
However much you try, the way to proceed remains unclear!
To alleviate this sense of frustration, listen to the chirping cicadas.

Ox-Herding Poem

WAKE UP!

The story goes that one day Suzuki Roshi, the great teacher of Buddhism, walked into his classroom and clapped his hands loudly. He shouted to his class, "Wake up!"

As we examine the long story of evolution, hopefully we can see that we are but one species with an important part to play on life's stage. Wisdom suggests that we come to realize that however much we consider humanity to be a key factor in the broad scheme of the earth's evolution, the simple truth is that we are a very recent development in the differentiation of species. We learn every day about species of plants and animals endangered or pushed into extinction.

It is possible that we can respond to the narrative of evolutionary history by romanticizing our progress, posturing the epochs of human participation as achievements and wondrous accomplishments. In many cases, our progress and achievements have been stellar – producing convenience, cure, and benefit for many who would otherwise have perished or survived in misery. A key difference between ancient and contemporary cultures is

made visible in the architecture. Where the ancients sought to import or bring down the divine gods and goddesses to the earth, our tall skyscrapers and church spires dramatically point as much to our success in developing new building materials and construction techniques as to our pride in reaching up to the heavens from the earth – exporting and punctuating ourselves so that everyone – including the gods – can see us.

However, when we look deeply at our own physical makeup, at the constitution of our bodies, and at our material world, it soon becomes apparent that we are the stuff of the stars. Our animation, our gift of life, comes from the soul – so unfathomable that we can really only determine the soul's existence in the empty spaces among the appearances of existence. Not here, not there – but somewhere between both and all. Perhaps we should respond by standing in awe that we even exist, somewhere between the starry cosmos and the inner radiance of a Golden Rule. As we meditate today upon the conscious program of devastation by humans all over the planet, perhaps we could imagine that there might be another way of living as part of the planet's symphony. The music continues to play. Perhaps we should wake up and listen!

Contemporary media desensitize audiences to pain and devastation – whether the loss or injury is local or global. Because the far reaches of the planet have been brought up close and personal through the power and immediacy of satellites and television, the wars that were once fought days and continents away from home now take place on the living room television set. Films, television documentaries, and glossy coffee table books chronicle the elimination of species, the horrors of war, and the abuses that we humans foist upon ourselves and the natural world in breathtaking color and poignancy.

Understandably, in many parts of our modern society we are becoming more than a little oblivious to the true nature of what is happening both across the planet and in our own backyards. What does it take to see that death, devastation, and human tragedy are idolized as well as demonized by both the entertainment industry and the military-industrial complex? These themes are among the prime motivations for the characters and plotlines of our most popular movies and they serve as justification for allocations of personnel and resources in support of defense posturing. Beneath the ostensible purposes of providing distraction from the day's events and security from terror, the bottom line is that fear of death, devastation, and human tragedy serve to stimulate our political and economic systems.

Have our minds become dulled, our hearts desensitized, and our wills paralyzed? We are drawn to the well of images that the senses desire for nourishment, implicating our lives in vicious cycles where images of truth and fiction blend seamlessly, melding into one another. News and entertainment have become indistinguishable. It is hardly possible to pull ourselves far enough back from these perspectives to question what is really happening to us. Across the country and throughout the planet, children give little or no thought to using a handgun, often in service of the adults who should be loving and guiding mentors. Often preoccupied with the exigencies of survival – both personal and professional – adults prostrate before the gods of progress, believing that economic activity is a sure sign, a leading indicator that the titanic ship on which they sail will remain buoyant.

It is the deeper nature of humanity to reckon its bearings between the responsibility to learn from the elders and the responsibility to serve and protect future generations. From the prodigal son of the Bible to Siddhartha's journey in becoming the Buddha to Phaethon's reckless abandon, the temptations of self-serving ego and materiality are archetypal and eternal. So, let us ask ourselves in light of the current moment, what can we possibly do to change the direction toward which we seem to be headed?

Phaethon is one of many stories the purpose of which is to dramatize what happens when responsibilities are ignored and abused, when pride influences human behavior. Pride is one way of becoming detached from the continuity of history, because the focus is upon the ego. When pride is engaged, we are turned from compassion and concern for anything except the ego. Not surprisingly, pride often identifies itself with product – something we buy or do or achieve. Thus, profit serves as a visual icon for pride – a wardrobe woven from the images of power, esteem, and security. Do we really think that it is possible that we can sever our connection with the past or avoid our responsibility for the future?

Humanity remains wrapped by instinctual urges – millions of years in the making – that continue to feed deep wells of anger, envy, greed, and fear. We paint images of violence, injustice, and terror into public display in order vicariously to satisfy those urges. Even if publicly we show dismay over those images, we indulge them privately with great satisfaction. Indeed, these images fuel the economy and as the Michael Douglas character of Gordon Gecko said in the movie *Wall Street*, "Greed is good."

Reptilian and mammalian brain stems continue to sway our behaviors and influence our political will. Yet in a nuclear age, if these instincts are the summation of being human, the consequences are beyond the possibility of rational consideration. Humanity is poised at the threshold of its own extinction. There must be profound changes in a short period of time unless the Earth is to become another red planet like Mars, barren of life.

The religion of love
        Is apart from all religions.
                The lovers of God have
                        No religion but God alone.

Rumi

METAMORPHOSIS

Metamorphosis is possible. Seers, saints, and mystics have through the years pointed out pathways of transformation that indicate that we can transmute the compulsion of our instinctual urges. They provide evidence that we need not be conformed to the world and that we can be transformed by a spiritual dimension of existence. Often courageous in the face of cultural momentum, these men and women have demonstrated in their own lives that the energy of our animal urges can serve as the foundation for bedrock spiritual qualities. Their experiences speak to the fact that love is the enduring archetype – that it is love that transforms our fears into compassion, connection, and curiosity. We learn that joy is more sustainable than the ephemeral pleasures of greed. The fury of anger can be calmed by trust and patience, yielding a quality of peace and wisdom that surpasses all understanding.

Though we can give thanks for the power of the instinctual urges that have transported us through millions of years of development to bring us to where we are, we now must "wake up" and recognize that these instinctual urges are not only insufficient to carry us into our future, they threaten our survival! A new quality of being is required, a new order of cultural engagement necessary.

To engage this new quality of being in the world will require change, courage, and some decisions – a daily decision to live by values that are higher and deeper than those intended to satisfy selfish urges. This decision awakens a new way of being in the world that is not only more satisfying, it eliminates the pain and disappointment of the old ways. Why? Motives determine the course of our actions. Conscious motives obligate attention and personal involvement. Unconscious motives rely upon a sustained lack of awareness, giving way to inevitable tragedy. As we extend our sphere of engagement to include others and the natural world, we can begin to appreciate the ramifications of our actions and to take responsibility for them.

We may wonder why people continue to indulge self-destructive behaviors and fantasies of self-delusion. Faced with the prospect of tragedy, why would a person forsake the delight of spiritual living? As Catherine of Siena writes, "The journey to heaven is through heaven."

A friend who is a professional therapist once spoke of a patient who was having considerable psychological difficulties and who disclaimed any belief in spiritual powers. My friend encouraged the patient to engage a process of stillness twice a day. Almost immediately, changes began to take place. The patient reported a newfound calm, expressed an improved quality of life, and saw movement away from the compulsions that had been the source of neurotic behaviors. Soon after, the patient practicing the simple ritual of stillness had engaged a new way of being in the world!

The patient's story is hardly unique. The real secret is that transformation is not the privilege of a few saints; it is the potential of the human condition. Transformation can be tested and observed in action. Whether it is the wisdom of the sages of China, of the rishis of India, or of the philosophers of the West, there are verifiable ways of developing a new quality of conscious awareness that offer sustained joy, peace, and love. It is not a matter of believing or being initiated into some new religion. Rather, it is a serenity and feeling of being at home in the cosmos for anyone who would undertake the moments of silence, knocking on the palace doors of the "Illimitable Superior Spirit," invoking humility, and seeking a spiritual universe that is beyond any particular discipline – and able to encompass them all. Thomas Traherne, the English poet, observed that "your enjoyment of the world is never right till every morning you awake in heaven, see yourself in your Father's palace."[110]

Phaethon's tragedy is that he was not introduced to an alternative. Phaethon had defined himself in relation to an all-powerful, absentee father and a well-meaning but ill-equipped mother. Phaethon's lot in the life of mythology has been to serve as a model for our own primitive ego drives that would seek to pattern themselves in self-indulgence. Since Phaethon's quest for identity was set in relation to his father Apollo, as a means of authenticating his divine parentage, he demanded proof from Apollo, who had given his word he would grant Phaethon's wish. Phaethon could feel the inflation taking hold. He desired to step into his father's shoes, if only for a moment: take the reins, drive the chariot, and feel like a man! Against advice to the contrary, he engaged the impulses for self-gratification for which he was completely unprepared – without guidance or instruction. However, lacking an authentic relationship with Apollo, Phaethon could only stand in opposition to Apollo and thereby mimic him. Blinded by his own desires, he lacked communion with anyone or anything – including the steeds that immediately discerned his lack of wisdom, "he does not know the horses' names." Communion provides access to wisdom and compassion. Resting in the silence of the depth of one's own being ushers in a profound sense of communion because when the mind ceases its chatter and the eyes close to turn inward, the oppositions that are the source of so many psychological tensions find resolution. Silence evokes humility because it represents the humility of that Spirit whose language is silence.

From the silence, we awaken into the world in a renewed state – ready to engage our personal experience mindfully and compassionately. So, as a signal of lasting value for our generation and for generations hence, let us clap our hands – just once, with impact and purpose. Let us humbly ask, seek and knock! Let us wake up!

Great Buddha at Kamakura, Japan

RESTING IN THE STORY

PHAETHON,
SON OF APOLLO

The sixteenth-century philosopher, Francis Bacon, once said that some stories are merely to be tasted, others are to be swallowed quickly, and a few stories are to be chewed slowly and digested over an extended period of time. The story of Phaethon qualifies as a story to be taken in imaginatively, reflected upon, and appreciated over a sustained period of time because the story of Phaethon is a narrative of universal significance. Because the ego represents the archetypal challenge for the psyche to cope with its identity and mortality, the story of Phaethon provides a window into the human condition.

Whether mortals yearn for immortality or superiority, the reality is that life for all of us – without exception – takes place within the boundaries of an apparent beginning and end. Myths of every culture articulate the challenges that humans encounter in dealing with the experience of being human. And each culture arrives at similar conclusions: it is wise and noble to love, express compassion, and worship the gods. It is unwise to be prideful, greedy, and envious of the gods.

If the universe can be viewed as a narrative, then a deeper comprehension of that narrative and communication with others about that narrative will facilitate our self-understanding and our relations with others, and will contribute to sustained involvement between people and the planet. As we observe the Earth's evolution, from the chemistry of molecules to the biology of life, there appear to be patterns that reinforce the idea of a universe narrative where the core theme of the story is the unfolding values of the universe.

Although there are variations from culture to culture, each tradition speaks to the origin and evolution of the universe as the sacred context wherein humankind flowers. Within this universal frame of reference, there is the potential for understanding and meaning. If one can imagine the universe as a text with meaning, it then becomes possible to ask, "How should we approach this text?" Some modern thinkers, such as Bertrand Russell and Jean-Paul Sartre, have viewed existence as empty of meaning. Nonetheless, their personal responses to the universe narrative involve moral discernment, authenticity, and acting in good faith in order to live "as if" there is a context wherein existence takes place. How, then, are we to read such a text?

It has only been within the last one hundred years with the abundance of scientific discoveries from astronomy to zoology that a scientist such as Albert Einstein could feel safe saying, "We're like a little child entering a huge library. The child notes a definite plan in the arrangement of the books, a mysterious order which it does not comprehend, but only dimly suspects."[111] In a library such as this, the student needs a method in order to read the texts. Although a certain level of technical expertise is required, an equally important component to reading these texts is the imagination, which draws from the deep inner wells of intuition and feeling – far different from the discerning qualities of rational thinking. As much a poet as a scientist, Einstein observed,

> Imagination is more important than knowledge. For knowledge is limited, whereas imagination embraces the entire world, stimulating progress, giving birth to evolution.[112]

The Death of Socrates
Jacques-Louis David (1748-1825)
Metropolitan Museum of Art, New York

The boundless power of imagination has the capacity to put us in touch with the essential qualities of our existence, to re-enchant the world we inhabit, and to restore connections with the natural world that are simply not available to the rational mind. Philosophers like Plato recognized the world behind the scrim of phenomenal appearances, the invisibles, as did Immanuel Kant centuries later. Steeped in centuries of rationalism, contemporary thinking is often littered with concepts, proofs, theories, and anxieties. Yet as any creative person knows, the imagination comes to us with an invitation to trust – for it opens doors to dark corridors, unexplored territories, and places where the soul fully opens to life. One cannot help but be enthralled in deep contemplation of nature, taking in the intricate structures of reality from the observations of galaxies to the movements of an earthworm. If indeed the universe does provide a narrative text, it would behoove us to ask: what is the narrative saying and what is the best way to approach and experience the numinous text of the universe story?   How do we take the story in mindfully and soulfully?

A few miles down river from Lee's Ferry, the Colorado River descends sharply through the Grand Canyon, revealing the Earth's history in the steep canyon walls. Layer upon layer of

sediment, each once the Earth's surface, chronicle the Earth's story. The uppermost Kaibab layer is more than sufficient to bury the entirety of human history. Beneath the Kaibab layer, millions upon millions of years of our planet's history unfold as the river continues its descent, taking us as far back as the Vishnu Schist 3.2 billion years ago. Few places on earth capture the Earth's narrative as visually as the Grand Canyon. Edward Abbey reminds us:

The great Canyon endures. The Canyon endures the trifling busyness of humans as it does the industry of ants,

the trickle-down erosion of snow and freeze, the cascade
of floods, the transient insult of the Glen Canyon Dam.
These things shall pass, the Canyon will outlive them all.[113]

To discover meaning in the natural world that transcends
utility and purpose, we must draw upon an appreciation of nature
that does not obligate nature to bend to our will. This requires
humility and deference on our part – awakening the senses as well
as trusting the imagination. The tension between the inner and
outer dimensions of experience has been beautifully rendered in
two poetic images, the Rose and the Fire, around which T.S. Eliot
constructs his poem, Four Quartets. The Rose symbolizes inner
contemplation, the flowering of consciousness. The beauty of the
Rose as an image of the soul in action brings forth a deepened
appreciation of both simple silences and things-in-themselves. To
hear the Rose speak, we must be silent, resting in the beauty of its
presence. By itself, though, the Rose is insufficient. The Rose must
be balanced with the Fire of an active, creative outer life:

> Ash on an old man's sleeve
> Is all the ash the burnt roses leave.[114]

Fire expresses the outer dimensions of life – the active,
moral, and context-laden experiences we face daily where there are
challenges, conflicts, and tests for the ego. Both the inner and the
outer dimensions of life are inspired by love and called together in a
cauldron of trust. Eliot observes:

> The inner freedom from the practical desire,
> The release from action and suffering,
> Release from the inner and outer compulsion,
> Yet surrounded by a grace of sense,
> A white light still and moving...[115]

Love, the Alchemical Mysterium, holds the promise and potential of a transmutation into something precious:

> Love is the unfamiliar Name
> Behind the hands that wove
> The intolerable shirt of flame
> Which human power cannot remove.[116]

Together, writes Eliot, "the fire and the rose are one,"[117] symbolizing two sides of one reality coalesced, each completing the other to make a whole. Together, they reveal the sufficiency of love as the heart of the universe.

In Jung's own life, he emphasized the inner dimension and crucial importance of developing the psyche through the process of individuation. Yet the fire in Jung's outer expression is readily apparent, as evidenced by the construction of his home on the shore of Lake Zurich and his serious commitment to painting and sculpture. Jung was as robust and active as anyone might imagine. Yet, he writes:

In the end the only events in my life worth telling are those when the imperishable world irrupted into this transitory one. That is why I speak chiefly of inner experiences. These form the prima materia of my scientific work. All other memories of travels, people and my surroundings have paled beside these interior happenings.[118]

I live my life in widening circles
That reach out across the world.
I may not ever complete the last one,
But I give myself to it.
I circle around God, that primordial tower.

Rilke

THE FOUR FUNCTIONS OF THE PSYCHE: GATEWAYS TO WHOLENESS

It is tempting to interpret history through the narrative story of the human species – traveling thousands of years back in time through architecture, ancient ruins, and pottery sequestered beneath the undergrowth where villages once thrived. But the human story does not begin to address the larger story of our cosmos – and while we may believe in our own significance or that the universe has been expressly created for us to explore and enjoy, the evidence and the myths that survive the ancient cultures strongly suggest otherwise. The humility of ancient cultures toward the cosmos has to a large extent perished with them.

But the cosmic narrative is no ordinary story, and must be read as much with the heart as with the mind. The story engages both the empirical and the imaginative dimensions of the psyche, both the scientific and the mythic aspects of our consciousness. Taken at face value, the story widens to encompass undiscovered galaxies beyond our own Milky Way. It deepens to reveal vast networks of complex sub-atomic organization that behave much as the heavenly bodies do. It is not unreasonable to ask whether we might be a small part of something far more expansive, just as the atoms we observe with our high-powered microscopes seem to constitute our world.

To gather our bearings in the cosmic journey, we must appreciate the four functions of the psyche. What do we mean by this? Quadratic formulations are a core construct of natural

organization: the four seasons, four phases of the moon, the four cardinal directions of the compass, and so forth. "Early in the development of human consciousness," British scholar Anthony Stevens tells us, "the psyche evidently acquired the propensity to orient itself to the physical environment through a tetradic arrangement of paired opposites."[119] Transformation depends upon bringing all four psychological functions into coherence, learning how to experience them in relation to one another, and how to find the depth of meaning in both the microcosmic story (the inner dimension of value) and the macrocosmic story (the outer dimension of fact).

Just after the breakup of his relationship with Sigmund Freud, C.G. Jung was drawn with great turmoil to explore the depths of his own personality, during which time he formulated many of his theories of the unconscious. Seeing the psyche as an expression of four psychological functions made sense to Jung. "It was Jung's empirical discovery," Stevens observed, "that the psyche expresses itself as a complete entity of balanced oppositions through the spontaneous production of a circular and tetradic configuration known in Sanskrit as the mandala."[120] By observing personality types in action, Jung realized that each individual houses a unique arrangement of four basic functions that orient the individual's relationships with the world. Through the functions of sensation and intuition, we experience both the inner and the outer worlds of relationships and things; through the functions of thinking and feeling, we evaluate or judge those experiences. It was Jung's contention that an individual's personality followed from the person's type, reflecting all four functions.

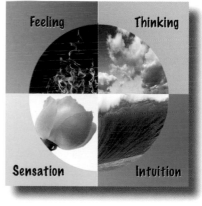

Jung concluded that people have dominant and inferior functions that drive the individual's psychological disposition that are constantly finding the best possible way to integrate. According to Jung, the Self is possessed by an inner impulse toward wholeness that is an autonomous function, a creative autonomy, in psychic development. This is the path that the individual intuitively follows to achieve psychological integration. The paths to wholeness and integration vary from individual to individual – which, although it is little consolation, explains why people often feel unfulfilled or experience painful neurosis when they live counter to their own natural disposition.

Self can be defined as an autopoetic impulse within the organism that motivates it to become what it is intended to be. The Self provides order and orientation within the psychological and the natural realms. "The notion of four entities as providing the basis of existence recurs again and again," Stevens points out, "not only in mythology, cosmology, religion, folk tales, and dreams, but in the course of evolution itself."[121]

If it is our hope to achieve psychological health or wholeness, the individual must learn how to develop the capacities of all four functions, in particular the inferior function, that function which is rarely used and, as a consequence, is generally under-developed and weaker than the dominant function. Within that development lies the potential for the numinous, healing experience of the Self. In alchemy, this is the *coniunctio*. Jung explains the tension that exists between the functions of the intellect and the heart, thinking and feeling:

> The intellect is only one among several fundamental psychic functions and therefore does not suffice to give a complete picture of the world. For this another function – feeling – is needed too. Feeling often arrives at convictions that are different from those of the intellect, and we cannot always prove that the convictions of feeling are necessarily inferior. We have every reason to grant our intellect only a limited validity.[122]

There is a path
No bird of prey knows,
Nor has the falcon's eye seen it.

Job

FOUR SPIRITUAL PATHS

Psychological integration has been a timeless concern of
the world's spiritual traditions – seemingly without
exception meted in quadratic expression, two pairs of opposites
creating tension, a virtual force field
within, emphatically declaring that
to invoke the gods or seek answers,
you must begin by looking inside
yourself with openness and sincerity.
In the West, the process is generally
considered prayer. In the East, it is the
tradition of yoga.

Thousands of years ago, the *rishis* (wise seers) of India were
already well aware of Jung's notion of the typology of personality
as they elaborated in their *sutras* or teachings the paths or *margas*
to psychic wholeness. It also appears that the prophets, the Desert
Fathers and Mothers, and members of the monastic traditions in
the West were equally aware of the importance of typology and
the four psychic functions, for they speak about transforming
work that must be done "with all your heart, and with all your
soul, and with all your mind, and with all your strength."[123] The
Biblical commandment of Matthew (5:48), "be you perfect even
as your father in heaven is perfect," shapes the core impulse toward
wholeness of every spiritual tradition on the planet.

Psychologist Robert Johnson observes:

> In the world of psyche, it is your work, rather than your
> theoretical ideas, that builds consciousness. If we go to
> our own dreams and sincerely work with the symbols that
> we find there, we generally learn most of what we need to
> know about ourselves and the meaning of our lives. Any
> form of meditation that opens our minds to the messages
> of the unconscious can be called 'inner work'. Humankind
> has developed an infinite variety of approaches to the
> inner world, each adapted to a stage of history, a culture, a
> religion, or a view of our relationship to the spirit. [124]

Inner work must be fashioned with one's own psychic
contents and materials, a process forged by the alchemists of
ages past as well as therapists of contemporary times. Although
a significant portion of the alchemist's time was spent in the
laboratory, the exploration continued inwardly by means of prayer
and meditation so as to maintain congruity between the physical
world and the divine powers.

The inner work of prayer went hand in hand with the outer
work. T.S. Eliot caught the significance of prayer in verse:

> If you came this way,
> Taking any route, starting from anywhere,
> At any time or at any season,
> It would always be the same: you would have to put off
> Sense and notion. You are not here to verify,
> Instruct yourself, or inform curiosity
> Or carry report. You are here to kneel
> Where prayer has been valid. And prayer is more
> Than an order of words, the conscious occupation
> Of the praying mind, or the sound of the voice praying... [125]

The four classic yogas of Indian tradition address and express all four functions of the psyche:

> Jnana yoga – thinking,
> Bhakti yoga – feeling,
> Raj yoga – intuition, and
> Karma yoga sensation.

The *Jnana* Tradition - Thinking

Jnana yoga is the pathway of thinking, the rational mind forming patterns of recognition, analyzing, choosing, and evaluating. It is "an intellectual, logical path of divine knowledge."[126] Rational thinking can be characterized by its reliance upon cognitive structuring, deep discriminatory processes, and proof. What *Jnana* yoga exposes is the inherent emptiness of reality, for it compels the individual to search for and locate what is real. By looking here, there and everywhere, it becomes apparent that the true substance of reality can best be determined by where it is not. This is known as *"neti, neti"* (not this, not that), a process that "puts aside everything belonging to *maya* (the phenomenal or measurable world of time, space and causation) as unreal, including all of one's desires and notions, until *brahman* (absolute reality) is left as the only reality."[127] All of our conceptual frameworks are recognized to be scaffolding that ultimately gives way before larger and larger dimensional perspectives. The idea is that the Real is immanent but veiled behind a world of appearances.

The *Bhakti* Tradition - Feeling

    Bhakti yoga is the pathway of feeling, of the devotional heart. This path moves through the ecstatic love of God to divine knowledge. In *Bhakti*, the student is led to intense feelings of devotion and worship of God, "wherein nothing exists save God and the consciousness of unity with God."[128] By the intelligence of the heart, emotional intelligence, the devotee is led to a transformative experience of Divine Union. *Bhakti* reveals selfless love to be a strange, but wondrous, attractor that connects all parts of the cosmos to one another. Love is the supreme revelation of the Divine in the universe.

The *Raj* Tradition - Intuition

    Raj yoga is the pathway of intuition, of meditation and inner silence. This path moves through deep stillness to divine knowledge. To achieve stillness, the individual withdraws all projections with the experience of "*turiya*, the supraconscious state,[129]" the fourth state of consciousness. The other three states of consciousness are characterized by deep sleep, dreaming and ordinary waking. *Raj* yoga recognizes silence to be the primary language of the universe, a language that betokens humility and is best learned by sitting quietly, motionless, and entering the serene state of awareness. Through the gateway of stillness, the individual learns to rest in the depth of divine being itself.

The *Karma* Tradition - Sensation

    Karma yoga is the pathway of sensation, of engagement with the world of physicality, with the world of nature. *Karma* yoga is understood primarily as selfless service in the physical world. It consists of unselfish conduct whereby the person offers all their actions – including the fruits, rewards, and results of their actions – to the divine. Nothing is expected in return, only the joy of serving a higher reality.

In the *Bhagavad Gita*, Krishna, advises the great warrior Arjuna, proclaiming:

> Yoga is skill in actions.
> When your understanding has passed
> Beyond the thicket of delusions.
> There is nothing you need to learn
> From even the most sacred scripture.
> Your mind stands by itself, unmoving,
> Absorbed in deep meditation.
> This is the essence of yoga.[130]

Eventually, through disciplined practice, the individual becomes an adept in all four yogas and understands the rhythms of inward meditation (the Rose) and moral action (the Fire), and that they must be nurtured together. For, as the *Upanishads* of India advise, neither one can be achieved without the other, and to court one without the other leads to inevitable darkness and tragedy. The *Isha Upanishad* tells us:

> Into a blinding darkness go they who worship action alone.
> Into an even greater darkness go they who worship meditation.
> Meditation and action – He who knows these two together,
> Through action leaves death behind
> And through meditation gains immortality.[131]

Personal maturation and self development follow a tricky, often peripatetic path, instilled as much by assurance as trust in the invisible forces. The narrow confines of any particular perspective create obstacles that are simultaneously self-induced and the nature of the perspective. A person's unique patronage of archetypes will coalesce – becoming integrated after a fashion – through all four psychological functions in the person's approach to the Self. Jung saw that consciousness begins to look like a mandala, a circular or labyrinthine process. He saw in yoga "many parallels with the psychic processes we can observe in Western man."[132]

Figure I (below) illustrates this parallel:

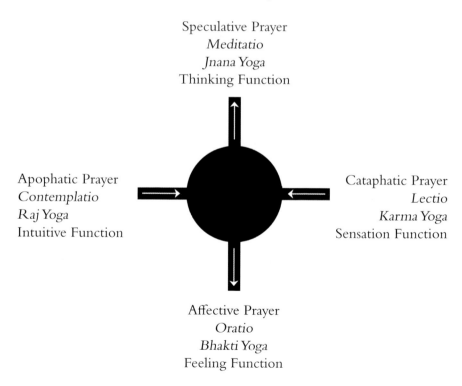

Speculative Prayer
Meditatio
Jnana Yoga
Thinking Function

Apophatic Prayer
Contemplatio
Raj Yoga
Intuitive Function

Cataphatic Prayer
Lectio
Karma Yoga
Sensation Function

Affective Prayer
Oratio
Bhakti Yoga
Feeling Function

During the years that Jung was mining the resources of his own inner world, his *prima materia*, he formulated his theory of psychological types, where he postulated the psyche as the synergy of the four psychological functions or dimensions. Jung saw that psychic development is not a linear path or sequential process toward wholeness but rather a circling motion of inner development that is constantly arranging all of the poles of psychic function to fit the individual, in the best way possible, given the circumstances and disposition. We grow and are nurtured by our experiences — just as we mature according to those archetypal forces playing themselves out within the Self in the context of those same experiences. Jung recalls his encounters and deep work:

> During those years, between 1918-1920, I began to understand that the goal of psychic development is the Self. There is no linear evolution; there is only a circumambulation of the Self. Uniform development exists, at most, only at the beginning; later, everything points toward the center. This insight gave me stability, and gradually my inner peace returned.
>
> I knew that in finding the mandala (the image of the circle) as an expression of the Self I had attained what was for me the ultimate.[133]

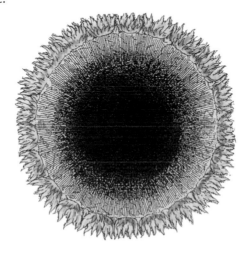

Lectio Divina means "divine reading."

Seek in lectio and you shall find in meditatio.
Knock by oratio and it shall be opened unto you in contemplatio.

Guigo II

THE TRADITION OF LECTIO DIVINA

In the prayer traditions of the West, there is an approach quite similar to that of the yogas of the East that illustrates how the four psychic functions facilitate our relationship with divine powers as well as among humanity. *Lectio divina* means divine reading. Just as there are four essential traditions of yoga, so there are four primary traditions of prayer. Thomas Keating, the contemporary Cistercian monk, is one of the principal architects of the practice of the Centering Prayer movement, a contemporary appreciation of the contemplative tradition of the West. During the

ascendency of the 17th and 18th century scientific revolution, also ironically known as the Enlightenment, contemplative practices were "brought into disrepute,"[134] leaving available only discursive methods of meditation, the way of the intellect, such as those taught by Ignatius of Loyola. Since the early 1960s and Vatican II, there has been a vast outpouring of material within the Christian tradition whose purpose is to foster a deeper appreciation of the fullness of the prayer tradition within the West. Looking deeply into Western prayer, we find, as with the yoga traditions, expression of the four functions of the psyche. On the experiencing axis of sensation and intuition are the *cataphatic* tradition and the *apophatic* tradition. On the evaluating axis of thinking and feeling are the *meditative* tradition and the *affective* tradition of prayer.

The Cataphatic Tradition – Lectio

In the history of Western spirituality, the cataphatic traditions can be most clearly observed in the context of the Eastern Orthodox Christian church. Within this tradition, prayer flows through the senses, to and from the divine. Contact with divinity is affirmed by sensation. Within an Orthodox church, the parishioner experiences the numinous presence of the divine primarily through the senses. For example, icons appeal to the eyes, incense appeals to the eyes and nose, chanting and rhythm appeal to the ears, and libations and sacred foods appeal to the taste. The involvement is orchestrated to engage the full repertoire of the senses in the present moment, connecting them with the Divine. The term from the contemplative lexicon that best describes this approach is *lectio*.

Lectio, "in the fuller sense, means the reception of the revelation, the larger book of revelation: the whole work of the Creator, his wonderful creation" through all the senses.[135] *Lectio* bridges our awareness not only to the revelatory power contained within the written word of various scriptures, but also connects to what the medieval theologian Thomas Aquinas regarded as the second book of sacred scripture, the world of nature, the cosmos itself. *Lectio* is conventionally viewed as the sacred vestibule to consciousness through the eyes – regarded as the windows of the soul – through reading of scripture, both written and natural. Ralph Waldo Emerson bathed in the numinosity of creation at his home near to the north shore of Walden Pond, arguably made much

more famous when Emerson enabled his friend, Henry David Thoreau, to live at Walden Pond. Walt Whitman found substance in both fields of flowers and leaves of grass, affirming the presence of the divine on Earth. Annie Dillard continues the tradition of reading nature for wisdom, writing in the *Pilgrim at Tinker Creek*:

The universe was not made in jest but in solemn incomprehensible earnest. By a power that is unfathomably secret, and holy, and fleet. There is nothing to be done about it, but ignore it, or see.[136]

Jesus says: "He who has ears, let him hear."[137] What is this seeing that Annie Dillard is talking about, or this hearing that Jesus refers to? Dillard speaks like a modern-day prophet who is pointing to the substance before our eyes and beckoning us to see through the superficial to the underlying sacred nature. Jesus knew that everyone near to him was hearing his words, but he also realized that the deeper truths of his parables were not heard by those deafened by prejudiced intolerance. The implication is that with a shift in consciousness, individuals evolve both their understanding and their experience. It is not what we see or hear but how. We see and hear what matters most. By engaging the full capacity of the senses, learning to read and intuit the deeper nature of reality, we move past superficial phenomena — very often the stopping point of the egocentricity of the rational mind — to deeper levels of meaning, appreciation, and participation. Jung makes this point when he writes that it is "pointless to praise the light and preach it if nobody can see it. It is much more needful to teach people the art of seeing."[138] Within the Western traditions of prayer, *lectio divina* represents a method that offers "the capacity to listen at ever deeper levels of inward attention."[139]

The Apophatic Tradition – Contemplatio

The apophatic traditions of Christian theology emanated from the vast deserts, the home of the Western Christian monastic traditions, whose roots trace back to ancient Jewish spirituality. The *apophatic* traditions counter the sensate stance of the *cataphatic* traditions by the pathway of silence and emptiness. Evagrius Ponticus (345-399) is one of the earliest known exponents of the *apophatic* tradition. Evagrius refers to the "prayer of no-thinking ...prayer without images or ideas of any kind."[140] Apophasis is akin to *Raj* yoga, in which spiritual discipline carries the student through the door of intuition toward an experiential connection, gnosis, with the Self. This form of prayer or yoga transports the person to a place beyond thought, image and sound, perfect stillness. Evagrius believes:

> Prayer is the suppression of every concept. In your longing to see the face of the Father in heaven, never try to see any shape or form when you are praying. Blessed is the mind which has acquired a total absence of form at the moment of prayer.[141]

The *apophatic* tradition has a strong presence in the West within monastic orders. Within the last several decades, Thomas Merton and his students, including Basil Pennington, Thomas

Keating, and William Menninger, have reintroduced this tradition of prayer to the public ironically by extending the reach of the monastic community through conferences and retreats. *Apophatic* prayer is often referred to using the Latin term *"contemplatio,"* resting silently in the Presence of the Divine, consenting to the work of the Divine within to heal and transform the consciousness of the individual. Though thoughts, sensations, and feelings naturally arise during prayer, these impulses are not given any preference. The approach to the Self here is through the gate of intuition, through the language of silence.

The Speculative Tradition – Meditatio

The speculative traditions stem from a practice known as *meditatio.* Augustine of Hippo and Origen during the classical period and Thomas Aquinas, Peter Abelard, and Ignatius Loyola during medieval times were the forerunners of the speculative traditions. Emphasis was placed upon tapping into the discriminative functions of the mind as a crossroads of contact with the divine – serving as both a means and a method for constructing a foundation of reason for a person's faith. Speculative prayer provides a blueprint that supports a person's spiritual home, especially in the early years of Christianity as the theological minds of those days attempted to separate gold from dross, true belief from heresy. As part of the newly formed Dominican order, Thomas Aquinas was a teaching monk. For him, God was reasonable and rational. It therefore followed that God should be accessible through the mind's eye. Thomas sought to help others see the synthesis of the worlds of matter and spirit. As mentioned earlier, we learn that toward the end, Thomas had a powerfully overwhelming vision that caused him to put down his pen. He became disillusioned with his project of writing an all-encompassing theological treatise, his *Summa Theologiae*, realizing his knowledge and rational vision were severely limited.

In the monastic traditions, the practice of *meditatio* is a simple concept. It is thought associated with assent – the evaluation of *lectio* into an assent of faith capable of experiencing the divine powers within. The idea is for prayer and relationship with God to make sense. In the nineteenth century, John Henry Cardinal Newman saw this distinction: "What this *meditatio* does is to change a notional assent into a real assent."[142] As the individual experiences the divine either through the senses (*lectio*) or intuition (*contemplatio*), the numinous contact translates into a host of ideas that form a scaffolding of belief. Belief commences as notional assent and is translated into a deep and abiding faith, real assent, in meditation. "As we assimilate that experience through meditation (*meditatio*) our whole being comes to respond to them. We move to real assent."[143]

The Affective Tradition – Oratio

The affective tradition, or the prayer of the feeling heart, is known as *oratio*. Affective prayer is often what most people imagine when considering prayer. It is a discursive prayer during which the mind reaches out to the divine through feeling, through the affect and intelligence of the heart. *Oratio*, according to Basil Pennington, "bursts out more and more constantly as the reality of our assent deepens and we more fully perceive the revelation of the Creator and creative Love in all that we encounter."[144]

Circumambulation

In both Western and
Eastern spiritual approaches,
and in archetypal
psychology, the movement
toward wholeness is circular
and peripatetic. Both the
mandala and the walking
labyrinth give symbolic
expression to circular

movement. Navigating with an internal compass that takes its
bearings and coordinates from the divine, the soul moves first this
way, then that way on its journey to the divine, the Self. Each and
every station is essential to the journey. Guigo II, the thirteenth-
century Carthusian monk, described the approach this way:

> Seek in *lectio* (cataphatic prayer) and you shall find in
> *meditatio* (speculative prayer). Knock by *oratio* (affective
> prayer) and it shall be opened unto you in *contemplatio*
> (apophatic prayer).[145]

Jung writes about the import of a relational approach to the
numinous experience of the divine Self that resides within every
person,

> It is not ethical principles, however lofty, or creeds,
> however orthodox, that lay the foundations for the
> freedom of the individual, but simply and solely the
> empirical awareness, the experience of an intensely
> personal, reciprocal relationship between man and an
> extramundane authority which acts as a counterpoise to
> the "world" and its "reason."[146]

In the third century, Clement of Alexandria defined prayer similarly as "a mutual and reciprocal correspondence" or "inward converse with God." The core element of the spiritual journey is correspondence with numinosity, defined by Rudolf Otto as having an uncanny supernatural quality that may be "overwhelming, or gentle, as the still small voice,"[147] providing the sense that one is in contact with a reality that is "wholly other," beyond the normal thoughts and feelings of everyday existence. In a letter written in August 1945, Jung revealed that:

> The main interest of my work is not concerned with the treatment of neurosis but rather with the approach to the numinous. But the fact is that the approach to the numinous is the real therapy and inasmuch as you attain to the numinous experiences you are released from the curse of pathology.[148]

Numinosity grants the soul an opportunity to see beyond the narrow boundaries of dogma and institutions to a larger frame of reference that would be so bold as to witness similarities among sacred traditions, between the worlds of spirit and matter, and between soul and body. Becoming aware of a moral law within our psyche, written upon our hearts, provides the possibility of finding connections not only to other human beings but also to all the other-than-human communities of the planet. Consciousness of the starry realms opens the door to being a citizen of the cosmos.

What fills me with awe
Is the starry universe above
And the moral law within.

Immanuel Kant

LECTIO DIVINA AND COSMOLOGY

The tradition of *lectio divina* provides a distinctively Western approach to an established tradition of engaging divinity that is a new way of reading our story and a new mode of being in the world. *Lectio divina* acknowledges the limits of human awareness – which in and of itself creates humility. With humility, personal transformation, the expansion of consciousness, and the process of healing the tensions exacerbated by the ego become possible. Through the four psychic functions, *lectio divina* promotes communion among individuals by developing a depth and openness within each of us. *Lectio divina* facilitates individuals becoming authenticated in the larger story of their own existence. When individuals see beyond the narrow frame of their own personal, familial, and cultural frames of reference, their lives can be seen as strands in a complex, cosmic fabric. The practice moves the individual into a fuller awareness of the universe as being "a communion of subjects rather than a collection of objects."[149] It is this participatory step that our present time calls for. Berry writes:

> We begin to understand our human identity with all the other modes of existence that constitute with us the single universe community. The one story includes us all. We are, everyone, cousins to one another. Every being is intimately present to and immediately influencing every other being. We see quite clearly that what happens to

the nonhuman happens to the human. What happens to the outer world happens to the inner world. If the outer world is diminished in its grandeur then the emotional, imaginative, intellectual, and spiritual life of the human is diminished or extinguished.[150]

The practice of *lectio divina* offers immensely tangible results. First, it invokes a true sense of awe for the immensity of the heavens and starry universe, which is the first step to availing an enlargement of awareness, cosmic perspective. Second, cosmic consciousness awakens the sense of beauty, the wonder of material reality from the very smallest of its inhabitants to the very largest structures of reality, including the heavens and galaxies. Finally, the awe and wonder form the basis from which to discover and be transformed by the web of relations, the moral fabric that connects the macro with the microcosm.

In his *Ladder of Monks*, Guigo II (lord of Ravenna 1316–1322 and host of Dante Alighieri) describes each of the steps of *lectio divina* and how each particular step is integral to the others:

The first degrees are of little or no use without the last, while the last can never, or hardly ever, be won without the first. *Lectio* without *meditatio* is sterile, *meditatio* without *lectio* is liable to error, *oratio* without *meditatio* is lukewarm, *meditatio* without *oratio* is unfruitful, *oratio* when it is fervent wins *contemplatio*, but to obtain it without *oratio* would be rare, even miraculous.[151]

Thomas Keating writes that as a result of using *lectio divina* to read our narrative, "a different kind of knowledge rooted in love emerges," a knowledge which "supplants the awareness of our own presence and the inveterate tendency to reflect on ourselves."[152] This shift moves us from what Esther Harding refers to as the second stage of consciousness, wherein the individual is preoccupied with the simultaneous multiple instinctual needs of the ego, to the third stage, wherein "the ego is displaced from its central position, becoming relative in importance to the new center of consciousness, the Self,"[153] a move from selfishness to selflessness. This unveils a broader perspective than the narrow confines of our animal instincts for self-preservation, self-reproduction and self-gratification. Putting the ego in its place awakens a conscious reconnection to the cosmic narrative, which is a story informed by the Self rather than by the ephemeral activities of the ego.

Our cosmology expands from the narrow confines of self-centered egoism to encompass a vision of ourselves in relation to the Sun, the source of our material nourishment, even as the ego stands in relation to the source of its psychic nourishment, the Self. According to both depth psychology and the many contemplative traditions, entering the cosmic narrative calls for an hermeneutic approach that is relational, as much dialogical as it is logical. Martin Buber offers the core insight: "All real living is meeting."[154]

Historical perspective reveals that humanity cannot persist for long without a functional cosmology. Such a cosmology must in some way affirm the awesome mystery of "being" itself, while also confirming the best judgments of scientific inquiry. *Lectio divina* provides a doorway of appreciation into the numinous mystery of our universal home.

No wonder that Pope John Paul declared that *Lectio Divina*, Contemplative Prayer and the Little Hours are spiritual practices of paramount importance as we begin the twenty-first century. Within these practices lies the hope of a new mode of being on planet Earth, one that is mutually enhancing and beneficial.

Dante Alighieri
Domenico De Michelino
Santa Maria del Fiore - Florence, Italy

Gracious Apollo! In the crowning test
Make me the conduit that thy power runs through!

Dante

DANTE'S LETTER TO CANGRANDE

Early in the fourteenth century, the Florentine author
Dante Alighieri wrote a letter to an Italian nobleman,
Cangrande della Scala, who had asked Dante to explain
the third canticle of *The Divine Comedy*. Dante spoke about
an "ignorance of the masses which forms judgments without
discretion,"[155] in reference to how many people are not able to see
beyond the literal dimensions of the text. He suggests that each soul
is capable of greater depth. Dante asked Cangrande to consider the
following biblical passage:

> "When Israel went out of Egypt, the house of Jacob from
> people of strange language, Judah was his sanctuary and
> Israel his dominion." If we look only at the letter, this
> signifies that the children of Israel went out of Egypt in
> the time of Moses; if we look at the allegory, it signifies
> our redemption through Christ; if we look at the moral
> sense, it signifies the turning of the soul from the sorrow
> of misery of sin to a state of grace; if we look at the
> anagogical sense, it signifies the passage of the blessed
> soul from the slavery of this corruption to the freedom of
> eternal glory.[156]

Dante illustrates the four senses of scripture, *lectio divina*,
in his letter to Cangrande. The four senses express four levels of
relationship, each involving a deeper awareness, and each drawing

the reader into deeper intimacy with the Self.

Annie Dillard writes "that the one thing that all religions recognize as separating us from our creator – our very self-consciousness – is also the one thing that divides us from our fellow creatures. It was a bitter birthday present from evolution."[157]

Ceiling Fresco,
Galleria Borghese - Rome, Italy

Perhaps self-consciousness is more bittersweet than bitter, more epic than tragic, for the sense we have of the Self is cut from the fabric of the whole by our own collective hand. What this suggests is a drama of epic proportion, evoking pathos for the personal pain and suffering of existence, the collective fall from grace that cultures one and all mythologize, and the webs of profound meaning that emanate from people seeking to navigate life on their own. Myths assuage the difficulties of awareness and situate both the person and the host culture on paths for returning to a place of cosmic connection. Self-consciousness holds the capacity of the psyche to become self-aware, yet the psyche is challenged by the forceful drives of the ego. By looking deeply into the reality of our own self-consciousness, by seeing through the ego nature of self-consciousness, we become able to transcend the confines of the ego that is our first line of psychic defense, penetrating the surface to the depths of soul.

Thomas Merton, the monastic mentor of Pennington and Keating, points out in his meditative reflections that *lectio divina* opens up a larger sense of connection to the cosmos and the potential to discover our place in the cosmos. Like the ancient Greeks, Merton suggests that the whole universe populated with *logoi*, little words, that are bristling with the "miracle" of life and that are the expressions of divine communication in a universe narrative. Merton writes:

> By the divine reading of the scripture I am so renewed that all nature seems renewed around and within me. The sky seems to be a purer, a cooler blue, the trees a deeper green, light is sharper on the outlines of the forest and the hills, and the whole world is charged with the glory of God and I find fire and music in the earth under my feet.[158]

Merton's protégé, Thomas Keating, connects the four senses of scripture with the four aspects of prayer and the four levels of relationship to the divine. It is a circular process evolving inward and outward as the person engages the divine through prayer. Actively becoming involved in these stages of contemplative prayer deepens appreciation and understanding of the cosmic narrative, and insight that the hermeneutical enterprise is a relational one.

The four stages are illustrated in Figure II:

Lectio Divina	Senses Of Scripture	Prayer – Relationship
Lectio – Reading	Literal	Acquaintanceship
Meditatio – Reflection	Allegorical	Friendliness
Oratio – Response	Moral	Friendship
Contemplatio – Rest	Unitive	Union of Life

Fig. II. Four Senses of Scripture

Of the four levels of *lectio divina* Keating writes:

> The monks of the Middle Ages called these different levels the 'four Senses of Scripture.' The senses of Scripture are not four ways of discussing a particular text on a rational level. They are four levels of listening to the same passage. These are the literal, the allegorical, the moral, and unitive (sometimes known as the anagogical). Modern exegetes focus primarily on the literal sense of Scripture. But that is not the purpose of *lectio divina*. Divine reading as the monks conceived it was not done for the sake of information but for insight. When they gave time to *Lectio*, it was something special. They would start reading the Scripture (*lectio*) and when something struck them, they would stop, reflect on the text (*meditatio*), and then pray over it (*oratio*).
>
> They would move from discursive meditation (*meditatio*) to affective prayer or aspirations of the will (*oratio*), then to repeating the same aspiration over and over again, and finally they would experience resting in God (*contemplatio*).[159]

Merton, Keating, Pennington, and others point out individuals in the history of spiritual exploration who were transformed by the hermeneutics of *lectio divina*, including John Cassian, Teresa of Avila, and John of the Cross. Approaching the story of the universe at the literal level beckons understanding but courts a self-referencing utilitarian spirit because the relations fall back to the personal and subjective. However, when the universe is approached through meditation and contemplation, an entirely different relationship emerges – one that affects not only the intellect but also the senses, and one that piques our intuitive capacities. Keating suggests that a new mode of being is brought forth as new levels of consciousness emerge. Moving past the literal level of cognitive appreciation, the allegorical level emerges when we realize that the story is "about us; that our own life is mirrored in its pages."[160] The allegorical level progresses to the moral level "when we begin to put into practice and live by"[161] the story we are reading. In a very real sense we become the cosmic narrative – the story of the universe. Finally, the unitive or anagogical level is brought forth through the Self motivating and directing our thoughts and actions. The circular motion toward the Self has now been completed – and when we become aware of our completion, of our success in transcending the ego, the ego ironically is awakened in a moment of self-awareness, for psychic success of any kind is a wakeup call for the ego. The process of moving beyond the instinctual needs of the ego begins anew.

The goal of this process is what Keating calls "the transforming union," and what the alchemists call *coniunctio*. Keating writes: "The experience of the transforming union is a way of being in the world that enables us to live daily life with the invincible conviction of continuous union with God."[162]

Mysteries remain vital to the life of natural phenomena so long as phenomena are not frozen in fixed frames of reference. As we experience the numinous in phenomena, our lives are transformed. Jung and others have attempted to suggest that as we transcend the discomfort and threatening nature of uncertainty, we open up new avenues of psychological wholeness or freedom. The tendency to reduce or reconcile uncertainty can be a trap that while luring the rational mind into a cage of understanding, strips the life from that which heretofore had been cloaked in mystery. Reminiscent of Merton's sentiment above, Jung writes:

There is so much that fills me: plants, animals, clouds, day
and night, and the eternal in man. The more uncertain
I have felt about myself, the more there has grown up in
me a feeling of kinship with all things.[163]

Alchemy offers unique access to the collective unconscious
– a bridge over the impasse between our rational thought processes
and the physical world. "Ancient alchemists," Ginette Paris points
out, "were unequalled at suggesting metaphors for the invisible
processes of the psyche. They saw that any maturation process
demands an impeccable sense of: a) the right substance, b) the right
timing, and c) the right intensity."[164]

When brought together, the three fundamental principles of
cosmogensis – communion, differentiation, and autopoesis – create
the right climate to deepen awareness of the mysteries surrounding
us.

You must prove yourself
You must pass through the four chambers of ceremony –

Hopi

PHAETHON REBORN

The Hopi Indian tradition tells us a story similar to the story of Phaethon with a twist that suggests a different outcome, shifting both the emphasis and the moral of the tale.

In Ovid's story, the reader is left with the death of the young man. A possible resurrection is implied. Do we dare imagine that

the tears of Phaethon's sisters, the Heliades, might soak the ground of his burial, bringing forth a new being out of tragedy? Will Phaethon return – wiser, transformed, different – to supplant the older pantheon of gods and goddesses and their outmoded values, as Zeus and his generation replaced the prior pantheon of Titans? Was the possibility of rebirth or resurrection written into the myth of Phaethon by the Greeks, or are we projecting it upon the myth? How comfortable are we with our own mortality? Now, let's look at the Hopi tale, *Arrow to the Sun*, that is recounted here by Gerald McDermott:

Long ago the Lord of the Sun sent the spark of life to earth.

It traveled down the rays of the sun, through the heavens,

And it came to the pueblo.

There it entered the house of a young maiden.

In this way, the Boy came into the world of men.

He lived and grew and played in the pueblo.

But the other boys would not let him join their games.

"Where is your father?" they asked.

"You have no father!"

They mocked him and chased him away.

The Boy and his mother were sad.

"Mother," he said one day, "I must look for my father.

No matter where he is, I must find him."

So, the Boy left home.

He traveled through the world of men and came to Corn Planter.

"Can you lead me to my father?" he asked.

Corn Planter said nothing, but continued to tend his crops.

The Boy went to Pot Maker.

"Can you lead me to my father?" asked the Boy.

Pot Maker said nothing, but continued to make her clay pots.

Then the Boy went to Arrow Maker, who was a wise man.

"Can you lead me to my father?"

Arrow Maker did not answer, but, because he was wise,

He saw that the Boy had come from the Sun.

So he created a special arrow.

The Boy became the arrow.

Arrow Maker fitted the Boy to his bow and drew it.

The Boy flew into the heavens.

In this way, the Boy traveled to the Sun.

When the Boy saw the mighty Lord,

He cried, "Father, it is I, your son!"

"Perhaps you are my son," the Lord replied,

"perhaps you are not.

You must prove yourself.

You must pass through the four chambers of ceremony –

The Kiva of Lions, the Kiva of Serpents, the Kiva of Bees,

And the Kiva of Lightning."

The Boy was not afraid.

"Father," he said, "I will endure these trials."

When the Boy came from the Kiva of Lightning,

He was transformed.

He was filled with the power of the Sun.

The father and his sun rejoiced.

"Now you must return to earth, my son,

and bring my spirit to the world of men."

Once again the Boy became the arrow.

When the arrow reached the earth, the Boy emerged

And went to the pueblo.

The people celebrated his return in the Dance of Life.

Phaethon and the Hopi story of the Boy bear striking resemblances: both stories articulate an archetypal relationship with the sun. Both speak of the immaturity and exuberance of youth, and the challenge of facing taunts about our cosmological roots. They share the speech of a journey to recover those roots. The difference in the stories, however, relates to how recovery will take place and whether the central figure will be redeemed.

In the story of *Phaethon*, there are no trials of transformation, although Apollo does his best to dissuade Phaethon from taking the chariot across the sky. Nor does the Greek myth speak to a spiritual discipline leading to a new mode of being. Similar to the Hindu story of the great warrior, Arjuna, in the Indian tale of the *Bhagavad Gita*, the boy in the Hopi tale must humbly enter a ritual that will transform him. In every sense of the word, the boy in the Hopi tale is woven deeper and deeper into the sacred ground of an initiatory rite. In the Hopi tale the boy endures the trials of the Four Kivas, each one a gateway through pain and suffering to healing and transformation. The symbol of each Kiva, the lions, the serpents, the bees, and the lightning are symbols of transformation.

St. Mark's Square, Venice, Italy

Lions symbolize the masculine, warrior energy of "the sun or a close association with light."[165] This energy of the animus can be employed for benefit or destruction. Lions are associated with courage and with the development of an attitude that is unafraid to court a trial of transformation. We may imagine Daniel in the den of lions or Shadrach, Meshack and Abednego in the den of fire. In many cultures, lions represent both wisdom and power. The lion is the king of the beasts, the animalistic heritage of our instinctual nature. It is regarded as the "ideal guardian of justice and the palaces of those in power."[166] In Christian symbolism, the lion is the signature symbol of the gospel writer, Mark, because his rendition of the gospel stresses Christ's royalty, his messianic role, God's deliverer. Throughout Venice, Italy, lions proliferate the architecture and art – symbols carrying forth the memory of St. Mark as well as the daring 9th century campaign that brought his remains to Venice from Alexandria, Egypt.

Serpents represent feminine energy, our chthonic, earth-based nature. In some images, the mythic Hermes, also called Mercurius, holds the caduceus with two serpents that stand for healing and transformation, the twin goals of alchemy, and a symbol that is still in use by the medical community today. The serpent transforms itself by shedding its skin periodically. It also promotes healing because its venom can be distilled for medicinal purposes. In India, the serpents stand for the liberating movement of the kundalini – a subtle feminine, spiritual force in consciousness through the seven centers of energy, the chakras. Basic instinctual energies of sound are transformed into sublime spiritual energies of illumination. It is a wise and powerful serpent that provides protection to the Buddha under the Bodhi Tree during his enlightenment. In China, the serpent is identified with the energy of Yin, feminine energy, and is closely related to the figure of Kwan Yin, the Buddhist image of great compassion. In the Americas, according to Joseph Campbell, "a serpent god, the Feathered Serpent [Quetzalcoatl], was recognized as symbolic of the power that casts off death to be resurrected."[167] In the *Bible* the Serpent in *Genesis* represents the seductive power that tempts Eve to eat from the tree of good and evil, bringing both moral awareness and the capacity for choice. Just as Hermes/Mercurius is the messenger and communicator, the serpent thus embraces both sides of psyche, sustaining vital flow among the relations of light and darkness that are as necessary for each other as day and night.

Bees symbolize the character traits of "diligence, social organization, and cleanliness."[168] On the surface the fruits of their diligence may seem to be the honey. But looking deeper into bees, we learn that bees form the connective strands in the fabric of agriculture. Bees pollinate everything from fruits to nuts, so a crisis to the community translates immediately to a crisis for humans. Beekeepers know the importance of good bee relations, mindful that honey and the gift of pollination easily outweigh a few stings. Bees have a highly developed sense of direction and can return to their hive from many miles away, navigating as a colony through an internal guidance system. Like serpents, bees have a potentially lethal sting that was also regarded as a medicine for healing. In North American Indian tales, bees were imagined as warriors helpful to ward off enemies. In the Kiva of Bees, the boy must deal with the collective aspects of his journey. Once connected to the masculine and feminine sources of power within, the vertical dimension of the journey, the initiate turns his attention to the concentric circles of social order and his relationship to that order, the horizontal dimension. Within the Bee Kiva, the boy learns how to work as part of a team, bringing forth the honey to benefit all, and returning home with the boon.

Lightning from the hand of Zeus brought Phaethon to his death, and from ancient times to the present, few other natural phenomena have produced the shock and awe of lightning. The Kiva of Lightning symbolizes the power of divinity. It is an immediate, ephemeral bridge between the heavens and the earth, conjuring deep fears in people as much because of its power and unpredictability as for its symbolism. In India, lightning represents the power of fertility. The illumination associated with lightning is a symbol of "enlightenment and sudden intellectual insight."[169] Thus, the lightening kiva represents the culminating trial of confronting our deepest fears and allowing these fears to be transformed into the insight of wisdom and compassion.

Like all archetypes, the lion, serpent, bee, and lightning are filled with, and characterized by, positive and negative aspects. Each manifestation of archetypal character is a gateway to the potential for blessing and new perspective. Each instance of archetypal expression is also imbued with the possibility of suffering and tragedy if not approached respectfully. Direct identification with the archetype, as we saw earlier, is a certain recipe for disaster. Ginette Paris tells us that what is required is to "serve the archetypal power."[170] In serving the archetype, liberation occurs through the numinous energy of that archetype seeding the evolution of the individual and by extension the collective.

As the transformation progresses within each of the four kivas, the boy is initiated into the broader collective – ready to serve the greater good. Now mature, his puer consciousness has transformed into the core of a person on the path to become a fully realized individual. Only by willing submission to the rites of passage and undertaking the appropriate disciplines of transformation can the boy come face to face with his real identity as a humble co-partner in the reflected energy of the sun. Without the mystery of the transformation, death of the psyche – and likely the person – will result.

La Chute du Phaeton
Jacob Jordaens (1593-1678)
Palais du Luxembourg - Paris, France

We learn from evolution that growth and adaptation are essential for survival. The key to adaptation is being relational and responsive – learning how to read the environment and respond to what it is saying. Alchemy suggests both the immanence and the necessity of an ongoing metamorphosis, an ever-evolving conscious adventure whose identity and character are the intimate expression of a transpersonal reality, the objective psyche, God and the gods. The alchemists postured this adventure toward wholeness as a fourfold process that has been symbolized by what they called the *Axiom of Maria*: one becomes two, two becomes three, and three becomes four as the One. In the yoga traditions of the East and the prayer traditions of the West, we can observe a fourfold process that illuminates the path of how to be at home in the cosmos and how to rest in the presence of divine reality.

To be responsible in the face of mounting environmental turmoil, individuals who can hear the call and respond with a program of mindful engagement will enhance the prospects of survival. As it always has, the numinous, archetypal nature of the cosmos articulates itself in such a manner that humanity can form a response. "For all of humanity," Michael Shermer writes, "it has been a long journey on the evolutionary and historical pathway to where we stand today, on the brink of triumph or disaster, survival or extinction. Which road we take depends on which moral choices we make."[171] The choice is ours.

Involvement with divinity, with the numinous nature of the universe, holds the potential for healing. Either a collective being that is whole will emerge or the story of the universe will continue without us. If we can integrate the spiritual nature of the cosmos with our own material drives and needs, the result will be a profound transformation. From a numinous experience, the rediscovery of enchantment with nature and cosmos becomes possible. Within the field of this enchantment, we become capable of reading and responding to the universe narrative with a depth of perspective that issues a capacity to see and to listen far beyond the biological limits of the physical senses. Here, there is possibility for wisdom and compassion to foster love, connection with, and awareness of all things and beings. This represents our hope of the current times and conditions in which we find ourselves.

The Fall of Phaethon
Johann Liss (1597-1631)
The National Gallery - London, England

CONCLUDING POSTSCRIPT

THE TRAGEDY OF PHAETHON
THE WISDOM OF THE MYTH

An epic or a tragedy?

Either way, the stage is set for an archetypal engagement with nature on a scale unprecedented. Whether the outcome lends itself to the Hopi version wherein there is transformation and blessing, or Ovid's version wherein there is great tragedy, depends upon the responsible choices of many individuals on a planet filled with uncertainty. In all likelihood, the results will be a mixed blessing.

Nature can and will survive without involvement from humankind – although today, the scars and heaviness of our footprints are evident. When addressing how the devastating effects of human involvement are threatening the planet, it should be readily apparent that it is our own survival as a species that is at issue. To continue our participation in the miracle of the universe narrative demands that we adjust our sails and chart a new course for human engagement with the world, for humanity is reaching the limits of the earth's ability to support us. "The essence of oneself and the essence of the world," Joseph Campbell once said with profound emphasis, "these two are one."[172] A new mode of being in the world, "costing not less than everything," must be distilled from the dreams we have of continuing to wake up in the world as we know it. To sustain the experience of the enchantment of this universe requires more adaptation than we have heretofore shown, a new way of seeing and listening to nature, reborn awareness of the underlying unity that is the wonder of the diversity of creation. Although perspectives from person to person and culture to culture may differ, they are each and all aspects of a single story of our universe wherein everything and every being in creation is integral to the narrative. Let us awake and behold the wonder of that creation!

The myth of *Phaethon* offers an incredible and imaginative lens through which to view the human condition. The ancient Greeks were possessed with receptivity to the divine nature of the cosmos and a deep wisdom that enabled the archetypal character of the cosmos to become personified in myth. It is understandable now that the pantheon of gods and goddesses took human form.

The populations of ancient Greece and Rome, however, would not have viewed the gods and goddesses as we now do. Rather, they would likely have experienced them as an interweaving of the interior landscape of the psyche and the natural world. Since they were not yet self-consciously separate from nature and the cosmos, the gods and goddesses reified their connection with the cosmos and were accordingly expressed in human form. Thus, Phaethon's exuberance, impatience, and hubris are relevant to us because we now seem to be suffering the same estrangements from the cosmos' sacred nature that the story of *Phaethon* articulates. His skewed sense of self is our own. His thrill ride across the skies is our own. And unless we recognize the archetypal pattern of the *Phaethon* story, his fall will be ours as well.

We are imbued with an innate craving to establish a meaningful sense of identity in an apparently untrustworthy and unfriendly universe – largely made untrustworthy and unfriendly because we have severed the bonds of participation and reciprocation that provided mythic cultures with a deep sense of faith and trust in the cosmos. Phaethon's kinship with the sun opens the door to the potential expression of the promise of divinity, that of being a light-bearer, a co-creator and partner in the ongoing process of evolution. As a species we carry the same potential and face the same responsibilities: to be stewards of the earth, co-guardians of the planet, to tend the land, the sea, and the air we breathe to nurture the web of life on our planet.

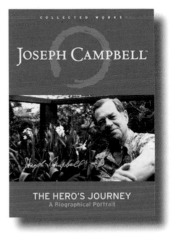

We may wonder about the use of ancient tales, such as *Phaethon*, in our contemporary search for meaning. Joseph Campbell put it succinctly when he said that, "myth is the secret opening through which the inexhaustible energies of the cosmos pour into human cultural manifestation."[173] Campbell showed how myths have a numinous quality with power to heal and transform if they are properly attended to and that myths permeate the human experience at our deepest levels of feeling and awareness. While the myths themselves may have morphed over time to fit the needs of particular cultures, the powers of myth endure.

In the lives of both ancient and indigenous peoples, myths reveal vast webs of interrelation between the worlds of psyche and nature – twisting the human experience of time and space so they conform and inform one another. Before and after, here and there, this and that – in myths, distinctions that make a point in rational consciousness become more than elastic, they enable the divine voices of the cosmos to be heard by the human ear. For cultures steeped in myth, there is a profound interchange between the psyche and nature, for the natural world is both alive and reciprocal – and mythic cultures then and now transact their lives in that reciprocity. To the extent the worldview of a culture and people is mythic, they will have feelings of reverence, deference,

and awe before the wonder of the cosmos. And, they will not realize it – it is simply who they are and what they do. Deeply seeded in the soul of the culture, myth enscribes their participation and intimate relationship in a much larger story, a story of the universe.

Dennis Slattery suggests the relevance of myth when he writes, "myths give back to an individual or even an entire people a felt sense, through images, of what matters and of what is at stake if what matters is lost, trivialized and muted." [174] Our universal narrative, our context, has been largely disassembled, de-mythologized, and demystified as the Western worldview during the past 500 years has increasingly enabled human beings to identify themselves with the powers of the universe. Personal empowerment has not only become a cliché, it has given license to cultures to export political will and economic perspectives under the guise of healing the seemingly less fortunate. Rather than situating ourselves within the larger context of the cosmos, we attempt to circumscribe the cosmos within the narrow frames of human understanding. We are surprised – indeed, offended – when the world does not bend to our economic will and scientific prowess. Yet today, the top scientists of research, government, and industry are beginning to revise their approach to nature.

Hope for a sustainable future is likely to be inversely related to our will and determination to continue down the path of excessive material consumption and abuse to nature. The signs on the road certainly indicate that the Earth cannot sustain the continued increase in population, the depletion of its natural resources, and the violations to sea, land, and air. As recently as 2008, Pope Benedict XVI declared environmental pollution to be a sin. An offense against God, said senior Vatican official Msgr. Gianfranco Girotti, "is not only stealing or coveting another man's wife, it is also destroying the environment." The reach of the mandate to curb sin was extended to include working for or with companies that contribute to pollution. "If yesterday sin had a rather individualistic dimension," Girotti said with emphasis, "today it has an impact and resonance that is above all social, because of the great phenomenon of globalization."[175]

If it is not already resisting our appeals to provide support for the human enterprise, the Earth may soon rebel against our continued efforts to impose human will on the processes that are the Earth's way of articulating itself. It seems that we have little choice except to relocate ourselves within an awareness of the universal nature of the psyche – and even if the path is filled with uncertainty, trust that in the long run the divine hand of nature will nurture us back to health and well-being. Human conceptions of nature have transformed the wonder of nature into a projection of the human species. Even if done unwittingly and with the noblest of intentions, the result has been to strip soul from the universe, turning the world from a place of enchantment to a world held in place by our narcissism. Does the universe have a soul? Psychologist Lionel Corbett offers this perspective:

> To assert the unity of psyche and nature is to repair a split which has bedeviled our culture. Unlike pre-technological societies (indigenous peoples) which viewed the earth as sacred, in our culture an apparent gap has emerged between the spiritual and material realms. When we experience the numinosum in the wilderness, we are not 'projecting' onto nature something that is actually inside ourselves; we are experiencing the reality of the continuity of the Self across the barrier of the skin.[176]

The apparent loss of soul, numinosity, or sacred nature from the world may have been a necessary aspect of the process of psychic development. Everything comes at a price. There is little doubt humankind would have advanced its myriad of cultural doctrines and progressed technologically had there never been differentiation between the conscious and unconscious aspects of psyche. Richard Tarnas writes of this development:

The disenchanting strategy can be said to have served well the purposes of its time – to differentiate the self, to empower the human subject, to liberate human experience of the world from the unquestioned pregiven structures of meaning and purpose inherited from tradition and enforced by external authority. It provided a powerful new basis for criticism and defiance of established belief systems that often inhibited human autonomy.

Tarnas goes on to write that,

We must awaken to and overcome the great hidden anthropocentric projection that has virtually defined the modern mind: the pervasive projection of soullessness onto the cosmos by the modern self's own will to power.[177]

Many of us are experiencing this as a dark moment in history. Our ways of living and our means of personal and cultural identification are in jeopardy. As the cartoon characters through the years have trumpeted, the world does seem to be coming to an end. And understandably, it seems personal, deeply painful, and even horrifying. The titanic ship of presumptuous pride seems to have run aground, no longer buoyant on the seas of opportunity.

Will we find joy in our time? Can we see a greater purpose in the events unfolding? Can we appreciate that a new beginning is emerging? Joseph Campbell often spoke of the need to see the earth as a symbol

at the heart of a new mythic self-understanding of our culture.
Perhaps, in Copernican fashion, the luminescent Sun in its relation
to Planet Earth could serve as the center of a new mythic awareness.
The stars might be seen as jewels in the night – once again calling
forth our dreams and imagination. Such a perspective is indeed
an invitation to cosmic consciousness, an intimate awareness of
our place in an ordered universe that carries an epochal story of
evolutionary adventure at its heart.

In her rendition of Ovid's *Metamorphoses*, Mary
Zimmerman has the psychotherapist speak thus after witnessing the
destruction wrought by Phaethon:

It has been said that the myth is a
public dream, dreams are private
myths. Unfortunately we give
our mythic side scant attention
these days. As a result, a great
deal escapes us and we no longer
understand our own actions. So
it remains important and salutary
to speak not only of the rational
and easily understood, but also of
the enigmatic things: the irrational
and ambiguous. To speak both
privately and publicly. [178]

So myths like *Phaethon*, *Sisyphus*, and countless heroes
such as Hercules, Theseus, Achilles, and Odysseus teach us about
ourselves, our drives and motivations, and our options to chart our
course for life on the planet. Today, a new kind of hero is required:
one willing to plumb the inner regions of the soul, to seek out
the dragons and predators roaming in the labyrinths of the human

psyche and to learn from these predatory beasts their reasons for being. We are entering into a new historical period, a time that Jung thought would take hundreds of years to complete and that we now are finding is imminently before us. Mystics and sages have referred to such a time in the spiritual journey as the "dark night of the soul," or more specifically, the "dark night of sense," a window of interior opportunity when we may more wholeheartedly identify with our spiritual awareness. We have crossed the threshold and we are now on the other side.

Three Ages of Cosmic Time

Thomas Berry and Brian Swimme refer to our current time as the Ecozoic Age, the successor to the Cenozoic Age of geological and biological time, as well as noological time. The notion of such ages provides conceptual scaffolding that is helpful in thinking about the vast, incomprehensible time spans of our planet's narrative. For us as a species, we might consider there to be three primary ages or periods of development relating to an evolution of human consciousness.

Millions and millions of years in pre-production, the first age, the Age of Biological Evolution, has our species under the spell of self-seeking survival instincts and urges inherited from our mammalian ancestors, whose development occurred during the Cenozoic Age, and our reptilian ancestors, whose development occurred during the Mesozoic Age, as well as deep-seated instincts from ancestors of a time much older, the Archeozoic Age.

The second age, the Age of Human Individuality, finds the development of a personal consciousness, an ego in which unconscious and compulsive primitive instincts gave way to the control of a new center of awareness, individuality set within a broader context of culture, and the advent of self-reflection and the exercise of individual will. This age demonstrates a dawning of the distinction between the subjective self and an objective world, a split between the path of the individual and that of the collective. During this age worldviews blossom, nurtured by spirits of adventure and exploration. Individual expression grows as the institutional restraints of art, science, religion, and commerce diminish. The project of bringing meaning to life takes precedence and fuels the engines of imagination and cultural growth. Under the control of the ego, cultures arise whose ethical codes are try this! and more is better. From the infancy of human development, our development has been a headlong, spiraling ascent to go further, have more, and become larger than life. Along the way, with few cues to reveal the limited nature of the world, even where there is evidence of moderation (such as the Buddhist Middle Way), cultures rarely expressed self-restraint in their development efforts. Often, like the people of Easter Island in the Pacific, cultures would drive themselves out of existence in the unchecked pursuit of prosperity and principles that underwrote the meaning and purpose of their lives.

The third age, the Ecozoic, is now just beginning. In the Ecozoic age, the ego finds itself increasingly under the control of a super-ordinate Self, the divine nature of the cosmos, that "Illimitable Superior Spirit" with a thousand names that include God, the Tao, and Brahman. In the Ecozoic age, humanity encounters spiritual liberation from the domination of our primitive instincts. In this age, individuals discover that the *kingdom within* holds immense moral power and compassion for others, including the communities of the other-than-human. We become capable of seeing the ego for what it is, resisting its impulsive and compulsive nature, and making wise decisions that favor the welfare of the planet. This new center of power unmasks the ego and is not threatened by the ego. As an expression of universal and reciprocal connectivity, it offers the soul a viable and joyful alternative to the myopic, self-

Michael & Dana White at Half Dome, Yosemite

centered point of view of the ego that is characterized by the many ways it is separate from the whole.

This new center of power is not unlike seeing something known to us all along for the first time where "the end of all our exploring will be to arrive where we started and to know the place for the first time."[179]   Our seeing now, however, encompasses the universe itself, which we discover to be a cosmos, an ordered home, and a genesis – an unfolding and uncertain adventure of epic proportion. At the *macro* level, laws such as gravity sustain the apparent order of the universe, while at the *micro* level uncertainty abounds. Our seeing becomes a gateway of personal commitment to a higher set of intrinsic values and communion through the paths of prayer, yoga, and mindful reflection already enumerated. And, our seeing involves a commitment to mindful engagement that includes respect for the environment, social justice for all species and biosystems, and love and tolerance for the differences and distinctions of life's multifarious nature. Indigenous people have always relied upon the quality of their engagement with the natural world, weaving the wisdom of nature's ability to reveal eternal truths into their parables and myths. An African proverb says, "the truth that was lost in the morning will be recovered in the evening."

Speaking of our Ecozoic moment, Berry and Swimme state:

> That the universe is a communion of subjects rather than a collection of objects is the central commitment of the Ecozoic. Existence itself is derived from and sustained by this intimacy of each being with every other being of the universe... Earth cannot survive in fragments. This is one of the most significant aspects of the emerging Ecozoic era... The well-being of the Earth is primary. Human well-being is derivative.[180]

Conveying this vision calls for a commitment to a mythic understanding of the universe in which the narrative is heard as the autopoetic voice of unity and diversity, which is to say, as a poem speaking itself. Once we hear the voice of the cosmos and see that we are a character in a greater story, the meaningful unfolding of that story becomes apparent. The scope of history and evolution begin to make sense when they are played out against a backdrop of humility. Then, as the drama of the cosmic narrative reaches full expression within us, it becomes apparent that we must take some responsibility for not only our own lives but for the whole of human history – for this is the soil in which the seeds of human enterprise have been sown. We must make a moral response to the welfare of the whole. Finally, in silence, it behooves us to experience the depths of spirit and the qualities of interbeing that pervade all existence – feeling the touch of time and space with our utmost sensitivity. Each level of interpretation deepens into the next and facilitates entering wholeheartedly into an Ecozoic awareness.

The primary concern of our time should be to get a grip on the primitive animal instincts that still dominate our thinking and feeling in both our personal and public lives. In an age of nuclear power and global terrorism, our Cenozoic awareness is simply

outmoded, dangerous to our survival, and no longer functional. The old pantheon simply must be replaced by a new cosmic appreciation. Radical spiritual transformation is necessary.

Jung remarks incredulously at our utter disregard and indifference to issues of spiritual transformation: "It is altogether amazing how little most people reflect on numinous objects and attempt to come to terms with them."[181] Jung sincerely wished every individual person could have an original experience of psychic healing and transformation. He writes: "Too few people have experienced the divine image as the innermost possession of their own souls."[182] His hope for the future was predicated upon the willingness of individuals to undergo a radical transformation by confronting the numinous quality of existence. Studying the traditions and arts of ancient cultures, Jung believed enchantment to be not only the oldest form of medicine but perhaps still the most relevant. He observed:

> The seriousness, indeed dangerousness, of the problem
> of individuation cannot be denied in an age in which the

destructive effects of mass-mindedness are so clearly apparent, for individuation is the great alternative that faces our Western civilization. There is only one remedy for the leveling effect of all collective measures, and that is to emphasize and increase the value of the individual. A fundamental change of attitude (metanoia) is required, a real recognition of the whole man. This can only be the business of the individual and it must begin with the individual in order to be real.[183]

The story of *Phaethon* serves as a mirror to reflect (as well as a window to see into) the timeless and ephemeral nature of the endless temptation to trade soul for transient thrills. This tragic myth is a powerful metaphor upon which to reflect as we imagine our way into the future. When we are poised at the crossroads of choice, will we have the presence of mind to listen to the wisdom of Apollo? Will we have the wisdom to truly master and not merely repress our primal drives? *Phaethon* is a lens to see our emerging human story mythically reflected in a meaningful universal story. The inflated character of Phaethon mirrors our own dangerous lack of insight, while his arrogant behavior is a window through which

Apollo and Phaethon
Giovanni Battista Tiepolo (1696-1770)
Los Angeles County Museum of Art

the devastation currently being projected upon the world becomes visible. The relevance to our contemporary perspective is not accidental.

In the myth, Phaethon undergoes a death – and a really nasty one! In the underworld, Phaethon encounters potential for transformation, a resurrection that may occur. Redemption is a classic motif of many hero stories in mythology and endures as perhaps a fatal flaw in our own storied nature. In much of our contemporary literature, movies, and art, the hero never dies. However, out of death, there is birth, and in the end, blessing emerges. We have only relatively recently begun to work with negative endings, paradox, and conflicted meanings in our modern storytelling. In some versions of the ancient *Phaethon* story, Phaethon actually reemerges in the evening – informed by the events, but nonetheless reborn to continue on. One of the many names for the great work (the *opus*) or transformation of alchemy that transmutes base metal into gold is coincidentally *The Chariot of Phaethon*. "The Chariot of Phaethon," wrote the alchemist Rulandas, "is one of the designations which the Philosophers have given to the Grand Work."[184]

The Chariot of Phaethon ties us back to humanity's evolutionary roots, while at the same time pointing to some undisclosed evolutionary destiny that implicates individual action in consequences that will affect the collective.

In both Western and Eastern philosophies, the chariot symbolizes the great vehicle by which the ego makes its connection between the worlds of matter and spirit. It is the vehicle of transformation leading to a new appreciation of the cosmos and an infusion of spiritual values.

Unus Mundus, One World, is one of the images that depicts this connection. It conveys the reunification of Apollo and Phaethon as father and son, divinity and humanity. This emblem suggests what might be in the culmination of the work of transformation, also known as *The Chariot of Phaethon*. It depicts the father and the son on top of the world of matter and beneath the planets and stars, the world of spirit. The illustration shows the connection of the son of the Sun to the powers of the universe. Humanity potentially stands in the same position of the son in relation to the energies and ever-presence of the Sun, a symbol of our connection to the greater cosmos.

One way of viewing the meaning of an individual life is through physical, mental, and spiritual growth. Accordingly, this frames a person's life and pattern of growth as a parallel to life and evolution of the planet. Esther Harding suggests this pattern of recapitulation when she writes:

> The development of the individual follows a path: what has been achieved only through untold ages by the race must be recapitulated in the brief space of a few years in every man and woman if the individuals of any one generation are to attain to a personal level of consciousness suitable for their epoch.[185]

The story of the human species is a brief moment within the framework of the 3.8 billion year evolutionary panorama of life on the planet. However significant, the merit and substance of the story will be found in humanity's potential to encourage wise self-reflection and compassionate self-direction.

The Fall of Phaethon
Peter Paul Rubens (1577-1640)
Museo del Prado - Madrid, Spain

If it is to continue as a species among the planet's other species, humanity must learn how to ferret its character from the cosmic narrative and to read its own script and story line in greater depth to see how it impacts the unfolding nature of the story. Our role in the drama of eternal time has taken on a significance the ancients could hardly have imagined. Yet, the story of Phaethon does indicate the gods are clearly communicating a warning to mortals.

If we can discern the broad outlines of the process of individuation with the context of the history of life on our planet, it becomes more meaningful then to re-imagine that process recapitulating itself in the life of each human being. The life of the individual is indeed connected to the life of the larger cosmos; the macrocosm finds itself mirrored in the inner reaches of the psyche of the person. Each reflects and impacts the other.

Moreover, the life of the individual takes on a larger dimension that, as it has flourished and expanded in scope, ironically and paradoxically places increased importance upon a deeper place of humility. For our actions will vary depending whether we view ourselves as interdependent and interrelated participants, kin to all, within the fabric of the web of life or separated from the fabric of life and free to do as we please, Phaethon's choice. In a context of interdependency, humanity becomes both capable of discerning a cosmic dimension to its sense of identity, *imago dei*, and responsible for it – which facilitates self-reflection and mindful engagement. When we realize that we are deeply and profoundly interconnected with all of nature and the cosmos, we consider the wisdom of our choices carefully – individually as people aware of the consequences of their actions and collectively as a species able to govern, implement programs, and tend to the well-being of the vast diversity of species on the planet.

Jung poignantly asks:

> So much is at stake and so much depends on the psychological constitution of modern man. Is he capable of resisting the temptation to use his power for the purpose of staging a world conflagration? Does the individual know that he is the makeweight that tips the scales?[186]

T.S. Eliot writes that in such a world as ours, with our very limited perspectives, "the only wisdom we can hope to acquire is the wisdom of humility; humility is endless."[187]

Apollo and Phaethon
Giovanni Mannozzi (1592-1636)
Galleria degli Uffizi - Florence, Italy

I give thanks to the single-celled organisms that struggled to survive the outrages of a volcanic world, to the trilobites and ammonites who existed within the turbulence of expansive oceans, to the amphibious creatures of old who dared to crawl out of those oceans onto the land, to the great reptiles who roamed the great shifting continents of old looking for a way forward, to the little mammals who survived being eaten by great reptiles, to the simians who leapt from one treetop to the next searching for greater security, to *Homo erectus* who braved coming down from the treetops to walk overmatched among the four-footed creatures of the earth, to the countless generations of *Homo sapiens* who forbore the slings and arrows of outrageous fortune and political power, and to my beloved wife and children who make this life an adventurous joy under the veil of a spectacular divine grace.

May we awaken each day
to unveil the miracle of existence!

LAUDATE DEUM!

Apollo Slays the Python
Eugene Delacroix (1798-1863)
Galerie d'Apollon
Louvre - Paris, France

REFERENCES

1	Miller, David: The New Polytheism, 82.
2	Carson, Rachel: The Silent Spring, 42.
3	Roszak, Theodore: The Voice of the Earth, 14.
4	Euripedes: Greek Tragedies: 98.
5	C.G. Jung. Speaking, 215.
6	Jung, C.G.: CW 13, 137.
7	Ibid., 12, para. 13.
8	Euripides: Greek Tragedies, 336.
9	Hobbes, Thomas: qtd in Copleston, A History of Philosophy, 33.
10	Russell, Bertrand: A Free Man's Worship, 107.
11	Ibid., 115.
12	Durant, Will: The Story of Philosophy, 246.
13	Cowan, Louise: The Terrain of Comedy, 169.
14	Toynbee, Arnold: Mankind and Mother Earth, 12.
15	Perlman, Mike: Spring Journal 1983, 91.
16	Jung, C.G.: CW 9i: 104; para. 189.
17	Paris, Ginette: Pagan Grace, 22.
18	Ibid., 22.
19	Ibid., 22.
20	Perlman, Mike: Spring Journal 1983, 92.
21	Rhodes, Richard: Dark Sun – Making of Hydrogen Bomb, 462.
22	Perlman, Mike: Spring Journal 1983, 94.
23	Teller, Edward: Memoirs, 20.
24	Ibid., 20.
25	Herken, Gregg: Brotherhood of the Bomb, 25.
26	Ibid., 25.
27	Teller, Edward: Memoirs, 6.
28	Rhodes, Richard: Dark Sun – Making of Hydrogen Bomb, 117.
29	Ibid., 270
30	Ibid., 460.
31	Begley, Sharon: Inside the Mind of God, 47.

32   Cole, K.C.: Mind Over Matter, 14.

33   Begley, Sharon: Inside the Mind of God, 32.

34   Ibid., 124.

35   Perlman, Mike: Spring Journal 1983, 96.

36   Ibid., 96.

37   Durant, Will: The Story of Philosophy, 103.

38   Rhodes, Richard: Dark Sun - Making of Hydrogen Bomb, 208.

39   Herken, Gregg: Brotherhood of the Bomb, 334.

40   Ibid., 334.

41   Ibid., 142.

42   Mitchell, Stephen (trans.): Bhagavad Gita, 43.

43   Ibid., 134.

44   Ibid., 138.

45   Ibid., 27.

46   Benjamin, Marina: Living at the End of the World, 42.

47   Hillman, James: Facing Apocalypse, 264.

48   Von Franz, Marie-Louise: Remembering Jung, video interview.

49   Brook-Shepherd, Gordon: The Storm Birds, 329, 330.

50   Von Franz, Marie-Louise: Puer Aeternus, 2.

51   Mandelbaum, Allen: Ovid's Metamorphoses, 13.

52   Rhodes, Richard: Dark Sun - Making of Hydrogen Bomb, 583.

53   Nunn, Sam: Carnegie Reporter - Vol. 5/No. 1, Fall 2008.

54   Roszak, Theodore: The Voice of the Earth, 27.

55   Barney, Gerald: Global 2000 Revisited, 7.

56   Ibid., 10, 11.

57   Ibid., 12.

58   Wilson, E.O.: The Future of Life, 23.

59   Ibid., 25.

60   American Museum of Natural History website, February 2003.

61   Kelly, Walt: Pogo. Hall Features.

62   Swimme, Brian and Berry, Thomas: The Universe Story, 3-4.

63   Ibid., 241.

64   Harding, Esther: Psychic Energy, v.

65   Ibid., 22.

66   Ibid., 23.

67   Ibid., 23, 25.

68   Ibid., 23, 24

69	Ibid., 2.
70	Ibid., 20.
71	Ibid., 13.
72	Blake, William: Auguries of Innocence, 60.
73	Hafiz, I Hear God Laughing, 7.
74	Blake: William: Auguries of Innocence, 60.
75	Darwin, Charles: The Origin of Species, 115.
76	Flint, Richard: The Earth and Its History, 8.
77	Fortey, Richard: Life, 53.
78	Wade, Nicholas: Fossils and Evolution, 99.
79	Knoll, Andrew: Life on a Young Planet, 3.
80	Schuchert, Charles: Historical Geology, 15.
81	Teilhard de Chardin, Pierre: The Phenomenon of Man, 51.
82	Fortey, Richard: Life, 308.
83	Teilhard de Chardin, Pierre: The Phenomenon of Man, 165
84	Fortey, Richard: Life, 105.
85	Wilber, Ken: Sense and Soul, 78.
86	Knoll, Andrew: Life on a Young Planet, 17.
87	Berry, Thomas: The Great Work, 26.
88	Eliot, T.S.: Four Quartets, 39.
89	Swimme, Brian: The Universe Story, 87.
90	Ibid., 72.
91	Ibid., 140.
92	Ibid., 140.
93	Perry, Whittall: A Treasury of Traditional Wisdom, 62.
94	Swimme, Brian: The Universe Story, 72.
95	Ibid., 89.
96	Ibid., 89.
97	Fortey, Richard: Life, 107.
98	Jacobs, Alan: Poetry for the Spirit, 237-8.
99	Edinger, Edward: Mystery of the Coniunctio, 12.
100	Harding, Esther: Psychic Energy, 19.
101	Ibid., 34.
102	Ibid., 57.
103	Jung, C.G.: CW 12, para.104.
104	Ibid., C.G.: CW 14, para. 279.
105	Alf, Raymond M.: Footprints in the Sands of Time, 89.

106   Jung, C.G.: CW 10, para. 105.

107   Soccio, Douglas: Archetypes of Wisdom, 136.

108   Tarnas, Richard: The Passion of the Western Mind, 328.

109   Jung, C.G.: Psychological Reflections, 52.

110   Traherne, Thomas: Waking up in Heaven, 17.

111   Begley, Sharon: Inside the Mind of God, 124.

112   Calaprice, Alice: The Expanded Quotable Einstein, 10.

113   Abbey, Edward: Grand Canyon River Guide, 27.

114   Eliot, T.S.: Four Quartets, 33.

115   Ibid., 5.

116   Ibid., 38.

117   Ibid., 39.

118   Jung, C.G.: Memories, Dreams, Reflections, 4-5.

119   Stevens, Anthony: Ariadne's Clue, 116.

120   Ibid., 117.

121   Ibid., 119.

122   Jung, C.G.: CW 8, para. 600.

123   Bible, Mark 12:30.

124   Johnson, Robert: Inner Work, 13-4.

125   Eliot, T.S.: Four Quartets, 32.

126   Schumacher, Stephen: Encyclopedia of Eastern Philosophy and Religion, 162.

127   Ibid., 162.

128   Ibid., 32.

129   Ibid., 284.

130   Mitchell, Stephen (trans.): Bhagavad Gita, 56.

131   Shearer, Alistair (trans.): The Upanishads, 15.

132   Coward, Harold: Jung and Eastern Thought, 5.

133   Jung, C.G.: Memories, Dreams, Reflections, 196-7.

134   Keating, Thomas: Open Mind, Open Heart, 22.

135   Pennington, M. Basil: Centering Prayer, 31.

136   Dillard, Annie: Pilgrim at Tinker Creek, 275.

137   Bible, Matthew 11:15.

138   Jung, C.G.: CW 12, para. 14.

139   Keating, Thomas: Open Mind. Open Heart, 20.

140   Pennington, M. Basil: Centering Prayer, 23.

141   Ibid., 23.

142   Ibid., 31.

143   Ibid., 32.

144   Ibid., 32.

145   Holmes, Urban T.: A History of Christian Spirituality, 54.

146   Jung, C.G.: Psychological Reflections, 353.

147   Corbett, Lionel: The Religious Function of the Pysche, 12.

148   Jung, C.G.: Letters I, 1906-1950, 377.

149   Swimme, Brian: Universe Story, 243.

150   Berry, Thomas: The Great Work, 200.

151   Pennington, M. Basil: Lectio Divina, 58.

152   Keating, Thomas: Intimacy with God, 41.

153   Ibid., 23.

154   Panko, Stephen: Martin Buber, 46.

155   Hollander, Robert: Dante's Epistle to Cangrande, 35.

156   Ibid., 37.

157   Dillard, Annie: Pilgrim at Tinker Creek, 80.

158   Pennington, M. Basil: Lectio Divina, 30.

159   Keating, Thomas: Intimacy with God, 46-7.

160   Ibid., 48.

161   Ibid., 48.

162   Keating, Thomas: Invitation to Love, 101.

163   Jung, C.G.: Memories, Dreams, Reflections, 359.

164   Paris, Ginette: Depth Psychology after Neuroscience, 150.

165   Becker: 179.

166   Stevens, Anthony: Ariadne's Clue, 348.

167   Campbell, Joseph: The Mythic Image, 288.

168   Becker, Udo: The Continuum Encyclopedia of Symbols, 38.

169   Stevens, Anthony: Ariadne's Clue, 146.

170   Paris, Ginette: Pagan Grace, 22.

171   Shermer, Michael: The Science of Good and Evil, 221.

172   Campbell, Joseph: Hero With a Thousand Faces, 386.

173   Ibid., 3.

174   Slattery, Dennis: Depth Psychology in the Field, 48.

175   Los Angeles Times, March 14, 2008

176   Corbett, Lionel: The Religious Function of the Pysche, 106.

177   Tarnas, Richard: Psyche and Cosmos, 41.

178   Zimmerman, Mary: Ovid's Metamorphoses, 67-8.

179   Eliot, T.S.: Four Quartets, 39.
180   Swimme, Brian and Berry, Thomas: The Universe Story, 243.
181   Jung, C.G.: CW 11, para. 735.
182   Jung, C.G.: CW 12, para.12.
183   Jung, C.G.: CW 10, para. 719.
184   Abraham, Lyndy: A Dictionary of Alchemical Imagery, 34.
185   Harding, Esther: Psychic Energy, 11.
186   Jung, C.G.: CW 10, para. 585-6.
187   Eliot, T.S.: Four Quartets, 14.

The School of Athens - Scuola di Atene
Raphael (1485-1520)
Wall Fresco - Stanze de Raffaello
Vatican City, Apostolic Palace - Rome, Italy

PHOTOGRAPHY & ILLUSTRATION CREDITS

The author and editor gratefully acknowledge the contributions of the artists and institutions mentioned below.

Cover: Ceiling Fresco Guido Reni (1575-1642)
         Casino dell'Aurora Pallavicini - Rome, Italy
         Photo: Dana White

Page   Acknowledgment

6   Ceiling Fresco - Artist Unspecified
         Photo: Dana White
8   Painting: Odilon Redon (1840–1916)
         Photo: Dana White
16   Self-Portrait: E Gard Jameson
18   Painting: Sebastiano Ricci (1659-1734)
24   Illustration: Michelangelo Buonarroti (1475-1564)
26   Photo: Ken Pomerance (Flickr)
28   Ceiling Fresco: Artist Unknown;
         Photo: Natalie Renaldo (Sweet Briar College)
36   Photo composite: Dana White using Flickr image

Phaeton sollicitant aupres d'Apollon las conduit du char du Soleil
Benjamin West (1738-1820)
Louvre - Paris, France